Actors'
AUDITION
SPEECHES
for all ages and accents

Jean Marlow

A&C Black · London

Heinemann

First published 1995
Reprinted 1998
A & C Black (Publishers) Limited
35 Bedford Row, London WC1R 4JH

ISBN 0-7136-4050-2

© 1995 Jean Marlow

Published simultaneously in the USA by Heinemann
A Division of Reed Publishing (USA) Inc.
361 Hanover Street
Portsmouth, NH, 03801-3912
Offices and Agents throughout the world

Distributed in Canada by Reed Books Canada
75 Clegg Road, Markham, Ontario L6G 1AI

ISBN 0-435-08664-2

CIP catalogue records for this book are available from the
British Library and the Library of Congress.

Typeset in Palatino 9½/12pt by
Rowland Phototypesetting Ltd
Bury St Edmunds, Suffolk
Printed in Great Britain by
Redwood Books,
Trowbridge, Wiltshire

JEAN MARLOW

Jean Marlow L.G.S.M., a qualified speech and drama teacher (Guildhall School of Music and Drama), is also an actress and writer with many years' experience in theatre, films and television.

From her early days when she worked with a group of actors and writers at the Royal Court Theatre and came under the influence of George Devine, she has played roles as diverse as 'Mrs Ebury' in Tom Stoppard's *Dirty Linen* in the West End, 'Doll Common' in *Playhouse Creatures*, 'Mrs Turner' in the award winning film *The Little Ones*, and recently 'Mrs Jiniwin' in the Walt Disney film *The Old Curiosity Shop*. She has also worked as a script reader for London Weekend Television, wrote the children's film, *Blue Doors*, and co-wrote *The Horror Bee Show*, which was successfully presented at London's Arts Theatre. She has a new play, *Phantom Lover*, currently in production.

She is Co-Director of The Actors' Theatre School, and it is her untiring search for suitable audition material for our students from many parts of the world, which has inspired this useful collection.

Eamonn Jones
Founder Director
The Actors' Theatre School

CONTENTS

Audition Speeches

Acknowledgements

I would like to say thank you to the actors, directors, play-wrights, casting directors, agents and organisations who have helped me with this book, including:

Brian Schwartz, of Offstage Bookshop*, who recognised the need and inspired the work, Richard Carpenter, Rona Laurie, Don Taylor, Gerry O'Hara, Nicholas Barter, George Cuttingham, Rumu Sen-Gupta, Peter Aldersley, Beverley Andrews, Sophie Marshall, Nigel Rideout, Wyn Jones, Glenn Conroy, Keith Salberg, Margaret Hamilton, Mark Dobson, St. James's Management, Geoffrey Vince, Natalie Haverstock, Charlotte Knights, Raymond Cross, Wayne Pritchett, Paul Peters, Peter Layton of the Drama Studio, London, Frances Cuka, Alan Haines, Geraldine Fitzgerald, Nicola Grier, Charlotte Atkinson, Reader Admissions Office, The British Library, Peter Irving, Library Manager, Victoria Library, Gillian Diamond, Richard Callanan, Helen Fry, Sue Parrish and Michael Hyde. Also Ronald Joyce and my editor, Tesni Hollands (who remained calm and cheerful under the welter of paperwork and permissions). And not forgetting my co-director, Eamonn Jones, without whom this book would never have been compiled, and the students themselves who tried out all these audition pieces for me.

* 37 Chalk Farm Road, London NW1 8AJ
Tel: 0171-485 4996 Fax: 0171-916 8406

To Clara Marlow
'A great teacher'

Preface

In a multi-racial society audition material is needed not only for actors and drama students from all parts of the country, but from all parts of the world.

I have sat through literally hundreds of audition speeches and have come to realise more and more the importance of selecting a suitable 'piece'. At The Actors' Theatre School we have had students from America, Canada, Australia, Hong Kong, Sri Lanka, Finland, many parts of Africa and the West Indies, as well as from London, the North of England, Wales, Scotland and Ireland. Many of these students have good Standard English, but others need audition pieces to suit their particular rhythm of speech. Even those with good Standard English accents often require material with a contrasting accent to show a wider range of work.

The hundred speeches in these two books, one for actors and one for actresses, evolved as I exhausted existing audition material and was forced to forage for new, or more suitable, speeches for both English speaking students and those from overseas. In these books, I have included speeches from plays translated into English, such as Anton Chekhov's *The Cherry Orchard* as well as those requiring an accent – Athol Fugard's *Hello and Goodbye* and Dennis Scott's *An Echo in the Bone*.

Each audition speech has been tried out by students at The Actors' Theatre School, either in class, at outside auditions, or in the London Academy of Music and Dramatic Art examinations (LAMDA). I have also avoided, as far as possible, pieces included in other audition books.

I hope that these books will fulfil a need for students from overseas, as well as provide fresh material for British and American actors and actresses.

1

About auditioning

From the moment you make up your mind to become an entertainer of any kind, you will find yourself faced with the Talent Contest, the Competition, the Interview, or – the Audition. I was five when I entered for Uncle Mac's competition for 'Young Entertainers'. A wooden platform with a red and white awning was set up on the beach at Felixstowe, and every day for a week I'd stood watching Uncle Mac and his troupe, in their straw hats and blazers entertaining the holiday makers. His big solo spot was 'Who Put the Oysters into Bed' and I'd learnt it by heart.

About six of us scrambled up onto the stage that afternoon and I was last but one. The winner was to be judged by volume of applause. 'Oysters' was a good choice. I was one of the youngest competitors, I knew all the words, and more importantly, I was in tune. The audience cheered when Uncle Mac brought me forward to take my bow. It was a marvellous moment. My mother was in the audience and I felt so proud. Surely I was the winner. But I hadn't bargained on the last competitor – a ragged girl of about seven with a dirty face. She climbed slowly up the wooden steps, took one look at the audience and then burst into tears. The applause was tumultuous. She was the winner and she'd done nothing at all – just opened her mouth and bawled. I couldn't believe it. I was stunned – bewildered. Looking back I can understand why she got the sympathy of the audience and the prize, but at the time there was no consoling a five year old who felt she had been unfairly treated!

How many actors and actresses have expressed that same sense of bewilderment after being turned down at an audition. 'I thought I'd done so well . . . they liked my speeches, I know they did . . . I even got a laugh in that comedy bit . . . What went wrong?' or students trying to get into drama school, 'Five auditions and I've failed every one . . .' or 'One more to go, but I expect I'll fail that too!'

You haven't failed

You haven't failed. You simply weren't selected. An audition isn't an examination or some sort of test to see who gets the highest marks. It may not always seem fair – life isn't fair – but very often you weren't what they were looking for. You didn't fit the bill.

A Musical Director who has sat through many auditions for West End musicals confirmed this. If someone walks onto the stage and they are not what the director is looking for, they will be politely sent away with a 'Thank you, we'll let you know'. The next artist may not perform so well, but if they look 'right' will very often get a recall.

A director is just as anxious to cast the right person as you are to get the job, particularly if he is involved with a whole season of plays. Does this actor look old enough? Should he resemble the actor playing his father? Will there be suitable parts for him in the next three productions? Should we look for a 'name' instead? It is not always the best actor or actress that gets the part – how can it be?

All the more reason to throw the word 'failure' out of your vocabulary. It took me many years and many, many auditions to conquer that feeling of rejection and realise that however good you are, or think you are, there are sometimes other influences, considerations, or circumstances beyond your control. The ragged child lurking around the corner, the television 'name' who will put 'bums on seats', or even the actor who has worked for the company before – a director may feel happier with an actor he knows. Providing you have worked hard and done your very best to prepare for your audition, you haven't failed, on the contrary, you've added to your experience and may even be remembered for next time. But let's have a look at the first audition most of us encounter when we consider 'going into the theatre' – the drama school audition.

Applying and auditioning for drama school

You want to become an actor and you've decided, quite rightly in most cases, that the best way to go about it is to apply for

3

drama school. You've contacted the various schools and asked them to send you a prospectus and application form. The prospectus should give you some idea of the courses offered and explain what will be required of you at the audition. Most drama schools in Great Britain are expensive and it is best to make sure you can afford the school of your choice before sending back your form and audition fee. Not all local councils, or in the case of students from overseas, governments, are prepared to assist you these days. One student was told by his council that they could train five engineers with the money it takes to send a single actor to drama school. Never mind. A few schools are now offering degree courses (BA Drama), and councils are inclined to look more favourably on these. You will also find some universities offering drama courses (BA Drama), but many of these are mainly academic.

In the United States there are very few vocational drama schools, such as the Royal Academy of Dramatic Art (RADA), or the Guildhall School of Music and Drama in London. Perhaps the equivalent would be The Juilliard School or The American Academy of Dramatic Arts in New York. Most drama courses are affiliated to universities, such as Yale, and are again very expensive. There are no grants available but you may qualify for a student loan. If you elect to go to drama school there are scholarships you can apply for, or you could approach one of the various Foundations for a theatre bursary.

When you have selected the school that has the most to offer *you* and you have sent in your fee and application form, do make sure that you have read the audition requirements thoroughly. You really should apply for more than one school as you rarely get accepted on a first audition, although it has been known. Audition speeches get better the more they are performed and there is no doubt about it, you develop a way of handling auditions. At your second attempt you will not be nearly so nervous and you'll begin to look around you and compare notes with others who are experiencing the same thing as yourself. Your first couple of auditions should, I think, be treated as a learning process.

Most schools require you to perform two contrasting speeches of about three minutes each, one of these usually to be a classic such as Shakespeare, Jacobean or Restoration – and the other a modern piece (in the United States they tend to lay less emphasis on Shakespeare), a song, some movement and improvisation. A few ask for *three* prepared speeches, although they may not always want to hear the third, and others send out a list of about ten speeches, ask you to pick out one or sometimes two of them, and contrast these with a piece of your own choice. All the speeches, and of course the song, have to be learnt by heart. It is amazing how many applicants think all they have to do is to stand up and read everything!

Choosing a suitable audition piece

Choose a character that is near to your own age and experience, unless of course you feel you have a particular talent or liking for playing older or younger parts convincingly. If your character comes from a particular region, or indeed from another country, are you capable of adopting the necessary accent? There is nothing worse than a poor attempt to sound like a Londoner, for instance, or a New Yorker. You may even find – horror of horrors – that the auditioner comes from there!

Contrast
Contrast is an important word in the theatre. Contrast keeps an audience from being bored – and hopefully an auditioner. Look again at those audition requirements and you will see the word 'contrast'. Contrast your speeches. If you have already selected something dramatic, contrast it with a comedy. If one of your speeches is Standard English or American, look for something with a different accent.

One of my students, Tina, was born in Yorkshire of South African parents, but had been sent to school in London. She has good Standard English, which she used for her Shakespeare selection – 'Isabella' from *Measure For Measure*, and her mother helped her with a South African accent for 'Hester' in Athol Fugard's *Hello and Goodbye*. She gained places in two drama schools. Another student, Canute James, born in Jamaica, chose 'Launce' from Shakespeare's *Two Gentlemen of Verona* and 'Dreamboat' in Dennis Scott's West Indian play, *An Echo in the Bone*, and because he can do a good American accent, 'Sean' in Thomas Babe's *A Prayer for My Daughter*. Good contrasts – a

Shakespearean comedy, a very funny scene with a lot of pathos set in Jamaica in 1831, and finally a scene set in a New York police cell where a drug addict suspected of murder is being grilled by a tough police sergeant.

If English or American are not your native tongue, there are speeches in these books that cover a fairly wide range of accents – the German tutor in Peter Shaffer's *Five Finger Exercise*, the Swedish Diplomat in David Hare's *A Map of the World* and the young black South African girl in *Have You Seen Zandile?* among many others. There are also plays translated into English, such as Henrik Ibsen's *A Doll's House*, where students from abroad can often find some affinity with a character and its speech rhythms. Marjo, a student from Finland, finds an affinity with Chekhov's characters and is a splendid 'Sasha' in *Ivanov*. She has also chosen a suitable Shakespeare character, 'Phebe' in *As You Like It* – how marvellously Shakespeare lends itself to all types and nationalities – and then contrasts these with a very moving 'Sophie' from Tom Stoppard's *Artist Descending A Staircase*.

Accents and ages

At the top left-hand side of each preface to the speeches, I have put the nationality of the character and/or if they have a regional accent. I have also mentioned where a play has been translated into English, or is set in a non-English speaking country. But please note, that although these plays have excellent speeches for overseas actors who perhaps still retain some of their native accent or speech rhythms, it is not a good idea for British or American actors to perform them in 'funny foreign voices'. As a general rule, you should only use a foreign accent if it says so in the script, or if your character is 'foreign' to the other characters in the play.

Underneath nationality/regional accent etc. I have indicated the age of the character. Some playwrights are specific about age, others give no indication whatsoever. In these cases I have simply put 'young', 'middle-aged', 'elderly' or 'old'. 'Young' is the most difficult to define, as it can mean anything from late teens to late thirties, or even forty – if you consider 'forty' as still young! It is important to be absolutely honest with yourself about your 'playing age'. Occasionally young people are able to play a lot older than their actual age, and make quite a feature of this, and I have known small thirty five year olds to play children of twelve or thirteen.

Read the play

I cannot over emphasise the importance of reading the play. You owe it to the playwright and to yourself. A student once said to me that she couldn't see the point of this. The character she was playing was obviously a young American girl talking to a crowd of people – it said so in the preface to the audition piece. What else did she need to know? 'But who is she speaking to?' I asked. 'Does it matter?' she replied. Of course it matters. It matters very much indeed. Your attitude to the character or characters you are speaking to alters according to the sort of people they are, their motives and your motives for speaking to them. Are they friends or enemies? People you love, people you hate, or people you are indifferent to? What has happened in the previous scene? What has just been said that makes you react in a particular way? Is your speech in answer to a question? If you don't know the question, how can you possibly answer?

John's speech in *Rutherford and Son* begins with the line, 'He knows well enough – you knew well enough . . .' Who is John talking to and who is he talking about? Why is he so upset? Although I have given you the answers in my preface to this speech, it is vital to find out more about the character's relationship with his father and his young wife. What circumstances have led up to this final confrontation?

You need to read and re-read the play. Gather as much information as you can about your character and ask yourself:

1) what does your character say about him or herself?
2) what does he or she think about the other characters in the play?
3) what do they think of him, or her?
4) what has happened in the previous scene?
5) what does your character want
   (a) in this particular scene?
   (b) throughout the play?

Each character is making a journey. At what stage of the journey are you when you are making your speech?

Sometimes, of course, the information given in the play is not sufficient and you may need to research further. For example,

7

Philippa was playing 'Lena' – the South African Cape Coloured woman in Athol Fugard's *Boesman and Lena*. The character is beautifully drawn, but Philippa not only worked on perfecting the accent, but realised the need to find out more about Cape Coloured people and study an older woman's movement. Her performance was a joy to watch.

You can make some unfortunate mistakes at an audition if you haven't read the play. Alison had a recall for drama school and was performing one of their set pieces – a speech of Mistress Quickly's from Shakespeare's *King Henry IV, Part II*. When she finished she was asked what had happened in the previous scene, and what had the character, Falstaff, just said to her. She didn't know, and had to confess that she hadn't read the play. What a pity! She had worked so hard and then let herself down on something so obvious.

Ian was asked to learn a classical piece and hastily picked out the first small speech he came across in the family's *Complete Works of Shakespeare*. It wasn't until a week after his unsuccessful audition that he realised he'd selected 'Julia' from *Two Gentlemen of Verona*.

If you are plumpish and over thirty it is not a good idea to pick out 'First Fairy' from *A Midsummer Night's Dream*. Believe me, I have seen this happen. The lady in question had learnt the speech when she was at school and hadn't bothered to find out where it came from or who was saying it!

If a play is out of print

If the audition piece you have chosen happens to be in a play that is out of print and there are no copies available in bookshops or local libraries, what do you do? The Victoria Library, Westminster, London has a very wide selection of published plays, and failing this, the British Library can be extremely helpful, 'application is open to anyone who needs to see material not readily available elsewhere.' For further details ring 0171-412 7677 (regarding printed material) or 0171-412 7513 (regarding manuscript material). Material may take several days to retrieve if it is not housed on site. The equivalent of the British Library in the United States would be the Library of Congress in Washington.

If the speech you have chosen is too long

The majority of the speeches in this book are between three and four minutes in length – an acceptable time for most auditions. However, there are occasions when you are specifically required to limit your time to two or even one and a half minutes. If you go over this time you are liable to be stopped before you get to the end, and if you rush it you will spoil your performance. Be bold. Cut it down to the required length. This is not nearly as difficult as it may seem. For example, Boesman's speech from *Boesman and Lena* can be cut by half, finishing on 'The whiteman stopped the bulldozer and smoked a cigarette. I saw that too . . .' and 'Private's' speech from *Philadelphia Here I Come* can be pruned considerably. If a speech does not reduce down easily, or you feel that by cutting it you will lose sense or quality, have a look through the play. The character may well have another speech lasting only a minute and a half.

If your speech has lines of other characters included

In some speeches lines of characters other than your own have had to be kept in. These additional lines should of course be omitted in performance. There are also instances in these same speeches where you may need to leave out a word like 'yes' or even a short sentence if it sounds obviously like a response to a question from another character, e.g. in *Night and Day* after Wagner says 'You never saw anything like it'. Delete Guthrie's reply, 'Yes I did' and also delete the beginning of Wagner's next part of his speech, 'Yes you did' and continue with 'There's a government press officer here . . .' etc. etc.

The song

Many students ignore this section of audition requirements, 'I don't want to be a singer, so why should I bother?' The auditioner usually insists that they do something and they proudly tell you that they stood up and sang 'Three Blind Mice' or the National Anthem. You are often required to sing in plays today, and in the United States, this part of your training is an essential. Even if you haven't a very good voice, the auditioner will appreciate that at least you made an effort. It is worth investing in a few singing lessons. Find a song that is easy to sing unaccompanied – you rarely have anyone to play for you at these auditions – and ask your teacher or pianist to put it on tape. At least you will be able to practise it in a comfortable key.

Improvisation

Some people find this very frightening indeed. I knew two students who passed their first auditions with flying colours, but on the recalls froze when it came to improvisation. There are many drama groups and workshops that make a speciality of 'impro', performing professionally in small theatres or pub venues and often inviting their more advanced students to participate. If you have never done any improvisation you would be well advised to join one of these groups. They can be contacted through theatre listings.

What do I wear?

Most schools tell you what to wear for an audition, particularly if they are starting with some sort of warm-up or movement sessions. The main thing is to be comfortable. If you know there is going to be movement and improvisation, wear something casual – tights, jeans and jazz shoes (the ones with the small heels) are easy to work in. Trainers can be a bit clumsy. I think women should change into skirts when they are performing their speeches, unless the character would be wearing trousers or jeans. It is best to put on a long practice skirt for classical speeches. You can always slip it on over your other clothes. It makes the movement easier and prevents you from taking great long strides, as we all tend to do when we wear trousers. A change of shoes can also be a good idea. A pair of heels can add that extra dimension to a sophisticated or indeed a 'tarty' character.

The men have an easier time, but it can often be helpful to put on a jacket if you are playing a very formal character and jeans and trainers look silly for classical speeches. I think dressing in black looks good at an audition, and you can always add on extra 'bits' for your second or third speech.

Should you have coaching?

A lot of drama schools say, 'no', they don't want to see a carefully drilled performance and I agree with them. However, I do think you need some help or advice from a trusted, experienced, actor or teacher. I spoke to a student who did Romeo's final speech at his very first audition. He told me that when he was supposed to 'die' he didn't know what to do, so he crawled away and ended up under the auditioners' desk. 'It was very embarrassing,' he said, 'with them both looking down at me lying by their feet.'

How competitive is it to get into drama school and what are auditioners looking for?

The Royal Academy of Dramatic Art (RADA) auditions between 1400 and 1500 students a year for 30 available places. The Principal, Nicholas Barter, looks particularly for commitment and trainability when auditioning younger (eighteen year old) students, not just those with nice middle-class voices and a few acting medals taken at school. He is also interested in older applicants (middle to late twenties, up to thirty years of age), some of whom have perhaps done drama at university, been a member of the local youth theatre, or worked with amateur companies, are prepared to re-evaluate their previous work and are open to being trained for a serious career.

Nicholas Barter commented,

> 'We aim to encourage initiative and develop individuality, not turn out RADA clones. My predecessor, Oliver Neville, used to say, "We are more interested in someone putting on a play in their front room, using their mother's curtains, than someone with a more formal background."'

I asked Rona Laurie, ex-actress, well-known drama coach and experienced auditioner, what she looked for when auditioning or interviewing students applying for drama school.

> 'The first thing I look for is commitment,' she said. 'I ask them "Do you want to learn to act, or do you want to be famous?" If the answer is, "Both," well and good. If it is, "I want to be

famous," I know they are not what we are looking for. The second question is, "Would you be happy doing anything else?" A strong "No" indicates a sense of dedication. I was once directing a group of drama students of which one was obviously lacking in concentration and interest. "What made you want to go to drama school?" I asked. The answer was, "I thought I'd give it a whirl." Consternation among the rest of the group.

I look for vitality in the work and something in the personality which arrests attention. Academic qualifications are not always necessary. Do you have to have brains to act? Not if you can act. There are "naturals" who seem to be able to act instinctively. But on the whole a sound academic background is an advantage. I am always impressed by the determination of students to succeed despite numerous disappointments at auditions.'

I then asked George Cuttingham, President of the American Academy of Dramatic Arts in New York the same question I'd asked Rona Laurie. His response was that,

'the overall policy at AADA is to admit all individuals who seem qualified artistically and academically as well as in terms of maturity and motivation, to undertake a rigorous conservatory program of professional training.

In the audition/interview, we give special attention to the quality of the applicant's instinctive emotional connection to the audition material.

Since good listening is so fundamental to good acting, we note how well the applicant listens in the "real-world" context of the interview.

Other criteria include sensitivity, sense of language, sense of humour, vitality, presence, vocal quality, cultural interests and a realistic sense of self and the challenge involved in pursuing an acting career.'

Auditioning for theatre, films, television and radio

After you have completed your drama course the auditioning process continues. Although, hopefully, part of your acting life will be working in films and television, it should be stressed that the most successful actors and actresses are generally those who have had a good drama school training and/or theatre experience. Of course there are exceptions to this. Models have been given leads in films and recently a casting director, interviewed in a magazine, described how she had discovered a marvellous looking young man outside a coffee house and asked him if he would be interested in playing the lead in a film she was casting. And we all know of a certain television series that was cast with a high proportion of non-professional actors! However, if you have had a solid stage training, have worked on your voice and movement, and had the opportunity of developing various characters and learning to play opposite other actors without falling over the furniture, you stand a better chance of gaining professional employment and staying in the 'business'. Even from a practical point of view, at the end of your drama school training you will be performing in front of agents and casting directors in your final productions, and stand a chance of being selected for representation or given the opportunity of auditioning for a professional theatre company. Offers of film or television work usually come because someone has seen you performing on stage in the first place. Very few film and television directors are going to take a risk on casting a young actor or actress, even in a small part, with no experience whatsoever – and the easiest way to gain this experience is via drama school and/or the theatre.

'Getting a start' can be a major problem, but by now you should have a fairly wide range of audition speeches, gathered together over your two or three years as a student.

Auditions for professional actors can be divided very roughly into four categories:

1) theatre – including musical theatre
2) films or films for television
3) television and television commercials, videos etc.
4) radio – including radio commercials and voice-overs

Theatre
Your very first audition could well be for a repertory or summer stock company, where a different play is presented every two or three weeks, sometimes monthly and, in a few rare exceptions, weekly. You will usually be expected to prepare two contrasting

speeches, so the director can get some idea of your range of work. Find out what plays are listed for the season. If it is a small company putting on *Rutherford and Son* or *Breezeblock Park* it is pointless giving them a piece of Shakespeare or a speech from George Bernard Shaw. Try to suit their requirements and choose two modern pieces – one comedy and one drama, with perhaps an accent to show your versatility. If you are auditioning for a company presenting plays in repertoire, i.e. plays that are rehearsed and then performed for a short while only, changed and then brought back again, the same thing applies. (London, of course, capitalises on this system with the Royal National and Royal Shakespeare companies planning their programmes so that tourists and visitors can see as many as four plays within a fortnight.)

Be warned! It is important to keep your audition selections 'brushed up' – or at least go over the words every now and then. Many of these companies expect actors to be able to audition at a moment's notice. A company looking for actors for *The Bacchae* expected a piece of Greek tragedy prepared in two days, and it's not unknown for a certain well-known company to telephone you at five in the afternoon and ask you to come in and perform a piece of Shakespeare the next day!

Frequently an actor or actress is called upon to audition for a specific part in one specific production. It could be a tour, a play coming into the West End of London, or in the States – a Broadway or off-Broadway production. This is an entirely different sort of audition, where suitability often counts more than capability. You are not likely to be asked to play the 'Witch of Edmonton' if you are only twenty-three, or 'Hermia' in *A Midsummer Night's Dream* if you are five foot ten, and most 'Falstaffs' are large in stature. You will almost certainly be asked to 'read' or 'sight-read' and will be judged initially on your suitability for the part, i.e. age, appearance, build, voice-range etc.

A word about 'reading' or 'sight-reading'
In theatre, films, television or radio, being asked to 'read or 'sight-read' for a part are one and the same thing. It means that you will be given a script to read that you have never seen before and be expected to give some sort of reasonable performance, or at least a good indication of how you would play the part. You may be given a few minutes to look through it, but sometimes

you only have time for a quick glance and then have to begin 'reading'. You should try to look up from the page as much as possible, so that the auditioner can see your face and also so that the words are 'lifted' from the page, rather than looking down all the time and mumbling into your script. 'Sight-reading' is a skill that can be learnt and practised until you can eventually hold a line, or part of a line, in your head and look up where appropriate, instead of being hampered by having to look down all the time.

Fringe theatre in this country, and off off-Broadway in the United States, has proliferated as many commercial and subsidised companies have had to close down. Most of these operate in pub theatres or in small arts centres. Several are experimental and of a very high standard indeed, but unfortunately not well funded, and 'profit share' has become a euphemism, with rare exceptions, for 'no money for the cast'. However, it gives actors and actresses who are not working a chance to be seen by directors and casting directors, and there is considerable competition for some of the better parts. Mostly, as in paid theatre, you will be required to 'read' and sometimes even asked to prepare a classical or modern speech.

Musical auditions can be a daunting prospect. In the United States, actors are expected to be 'all-rounders' – equipped for both musicals and 'straight' theatre. In the United Kingdom we tend to divide ourselves into those who do musicals because they can sing and/or 'move' and those who only do straight plays because they can't, or don't want to! Nowadays, more and more plays require actors who can do both, and it is a good idea to take a few singing lessons, add a couple of songs to your repertoire and perhaps even learn a few dance steps.

Films
A film director looks for a much smaller scale performance, and very often you won't even be considered unless you are very near to, or 'are' the character he is looking for. At a first interview you may be asked to 'read' and then perhaps 'read' again on video. The director will usually ask an actor to do 'less' not 'more', and sometimes it can be difficult to adjust to this if you have been working consistently in the theatre giving a much

broader performance i.e. using more voice, more movement and bigger gestures. If you are called back, try to learn the lines so that you don't have to keep looking down at the script, or better still, not look at it at all. As you get closer to getting the part watch that you don't tense up. Relaxation now becomes of prime importance. Enjoy playing the scene and forget how much you want the part – keep it loose and relaxed.

Television
You will more than likely be expected to 'read' at a television audition unless the director and casting director already know your work. As with films, you are mostly required to scale down your performance. Don't be hurried into a reading. Ask if you can have at least a minute to look through the part. Very often you will be given a script to take away and study and come back again a few days later. Here again, suitability counts more than capability, and you are sometimes only cast because you come from that area or part of the world where the action is set. This is particularly so with documentaries, or dramatisations of crime reports, etc.

Commercials
It has been said that the success rate for 'Commercial Auditions' is about one in twenty. 'Advertisers' like to have lots of actors to choose from, so it's as well to bear this in mind and not be too downhearted if you don't come away with the job! When you arrive for your appointment you will most likely be handed a script or story line and asked to study it in the waiting room until called. If you have lines to say try to familiarise yourself with them as much as possible. You will almost certainly be videoed, and remember your face is important – not the top of your head. These auditions can be a bizarre experience. Some years ago a friend of mine was 'put up' for an egg commercial. She was shown into a large boardroom with a long polished table, around which sat the production team and the advertisers. There was a pair of flippers on the table and she was asked to put these on and jump around the room saying, 'I'm an egg chick. Eggs are cheap this week.' Yes, actors have to be prepared for anything!

Radio

For commercial recordings and voice-overs, either on television or radio, you will be asked to 'read' – sometimes in an office, or in a small sound studio in front of a microphone. It may be for a specific job, or a general audition where your tape is then filed for future reference and played through when the company are looking for a particular voice for a particular production.

If you are auditioning for BBC Radio Drama, you are required to present two, preferably contrasting speeches of about a minute each. Auditions are always held in a studio in front of a microphone, with either one, or two drama producers listening to you in the sound box. You will be given approximately five minutes on tape and should use some of this time to give short examples of accents and dialects in order to show your versatility, although this is not obligatory. These have to be good, as if you slip up on an accent on radio, it can be so horribly obvious.

What auditioners look for

Who are the people who audition you for professional work in theatre, films, television and radio? They may be casting directors, producers, directors, assistant directors, writers – or even a combination of all these people. Usually a casting director calls you to an audition because he or she knows you, or knows of your work, you have written in and your CV and picture are of interest for a particular production, or an agent has strongly recommended you as being suitable for a specific part. Initially you may see only the casting director, and then be called back later either to 'read' or 'screen test' for the director, or perform a suitable audition speech. An auditioner is just as anxious to cast the right actor or actress for the part as you are to get the job.

I talked to a group of actors and actresses at the Belgrade Theatre, Coventry, most of whom had left drama school within the past five years. They all felt it would be really helpful if they could have some advice from the auditioners themselves. Older actors also thought this would be useful. I asked some directors and casting directors to explain their side of the auditioning process and give some tips on the do's and don'ts of auditioning.

Rumu Sen-Gupta – Joint Artistic Director of the Belgrade Theatre, Coventry:

'Some positive thoughts to remember when you audition . . .

1) What the Director you're seeing wants most of all, is for someone to come in and walk away with the part. They don't want to agonise and be full of uncertainty. They are, therefore, hoping the moment you walk in, that you will be the right person for the part.

2) When you are called for an audition it is because: something about you and your work has made you stand out from the rest. Directors receive increasingly large amounts of submissions from agents and individuals. The fact that you

have been asked to audition is no small achievement on
your part.

3) If you are asked to read or perform a piece you have an
   ideal opportunity to show the Director some of the qualities
   you have as an actor. It's not a performance that Directors
   are looking for, it's the potential of what you have to offer.

4) All directors are human (although they may not appear to
   be)! Human beings enjoy positive contact with each other.
   The more you are able to contribute towards an enjoyable
   meeting, the more the audition will feel like it's going well,
   the more relaxed and confident you will become, and the
   more the likelihood exists of your landing the part.'

Don Taylor – theatre and television director and playwright –
excerpts from his plays have been included in this book:

'Auditions and interviews are nerve-racking for actors because
they are laying on the line not only their artistic selves but their
livelihood. Rejection for an actor is always personal, in a way it
is not for a playwright, because body and soul are being rejected,
not something external that the artist has made . . . It is worth
remembering that auditions are difficult for directors too. I often
feel that the person most likely to get the job is the one that
puts me at my ease. After all, if you enjoy meeting someone,
have an interesting talk and some good serious work on the
play, you are more likely to want to work with them, if only to
renew an interesting acquaintance.

The director's difficulty, assuming he doesn't have a close
acquaintance with the actor's work, is simply that he has to
make a crucial judgement in a short time on insufficient evi-
dence. If he gets it wrong, and casts the wrong person, his
production will be doomed before rehearsal begins. All directors
know this, and realise that there are times when they just have
to play a hunch and hope that it works. To sum up an actor's
potential – can he or she actually act, or is it merely a question
of good reading technique, is the personality right for the part
as far as the director conceives it, will the process of exploration
go far enough and deep enough with this particular actor, or
will it merely be a question of a polished surface and no heart?

– in a brief meeting and perhaps a reading, is a daunting task. Very often a director might have half a dozen people, all of whom can act and will dig deep, all of whom are suitable for the part – not merely a question of looks, but of personality – and each one of whom will do it in a different way. Then the director has to consider making a working group with his other actors, and if that doesn't solve the problem, sleep on it, or in the final desperate analysis, simply toss a coin! I have never actually done that, physically, but I have once or twice done something mentally akin.'

Sophie Marshall – Casting Director at the Royal Exchange Theatre Company, Manchester:

'It is so hard to give absolute rules for auditions as it is all a question of taste, but in the end I think common sense and as much research as possible should prevail! So here are some pointers:

1) find out who you will be meeting and, if possible, the kind of plays they may be planning,

2) choose speeches which suit your age and type,

3) make sure you read the play from which your speeches are taken, so you fully understand the context,

4) perhaps you might prepare more than the one or two speeches required, so you can offer a choice.'

Gillian Diamond – Head of Casting with the Royal National Theatre for fifteen years and also the Royal Shakespeare Company and now Associate Producer of the Sir Peter Hall Company – also runs a course at the Drama Centre, London preparing the third year students for entry into the profession:

'Read plays carefully and choose wisely to suit your strengths. Have a variety of pieces and keep changing them, they quickly become stale and therefore uninteresting. Be imaginative; wear clothes to assist your character and chuck the trainers.

Always be natural and positive in interviews. Try and find out why you are being seen and do some research on the playwright concerned.

If you know what the play is to be, read it thoroughly. Don't plead lack of time, or lack of being informed as an excuse. Most people are nice and wish you to succeed, so meet them with a positive attitude. Never be grim. Try and be well informed and enthusiastic about the profession.

Remember that "many are called and few are chosen". All you can do is to come out knowing you have done your best – no regrets.'

Gerry O'Hara – has written and directed for films and television. He wrote the television adaptation of the mini-series *Operation Julie* and directed for *The Avengers*, *The Professionals* and other series. Earlier in his career he was Assistant Director to Laurence Olivier (*Richard III*), Carol Reed (*The Keep* and *Our Man in Havana*), Otto Preminger (*Exodus* and *The Cardinal*), Vincente Minelli (*The Four Horsemen of the Apocalypse*), Tony Richardson (*Tom Jones*), Anatole Litvak (*Anastasia* and *The Journey*) and many others:

'Casting for films, and to some extent television, often involves an audition and a video test scene. The director usually tries to establish a rapport with the artiste. Certainly a relaxed informality is the best approach on both sides. The director may have a number of parts in mind; or may be storing up ideas for future productions.

The video "test" is usually a two or three page reading of a script that the artiste has not read in full and is often asked to tackle with as little as half-an-hour's notice. It is a tough proposition, even if it is prompted by necessity.

If the part is contemporary it is probably wisest to underplay, raising the temperature under the director's guidance. If you start by overplaying it is harder to quickly shrug off that approach and drop down as it were.

Casting a horror movie last year in Israel – American leads plus local supporting parts – it was interesting to see how heavily theatre-orientated players approached movie acting. Several of the established players had acted in European and American films and television and were completely at ease with the technique but those with years of experience in playing the theatres and one-night stands were steeped in a heavier style. And, of course, they were not playing in their own language.

21

Here again the best advice was to underplay. The camera does the rest!'

Richard Callanan – Executive Producer, Children's Drama, BBC:

'Unlike the theatre, most auditions for television are for a single part so the producers have often a clear, if not blinkered, idea of what they are looking for. So the first job of the auditionee is to find out what they are looking for. This is not always easy. Established stars can ask for scripts in advance but most actors will have to get by with a garbled summary from their agent and perhaps a few pages of script when they arrive for interview.

The brutal reality of the process is that, again except for established stars, it is a buyer's market. Generous producers may have the good manners to disguise this power relationship but ignore it at your peril. This means that you must always be on time, or early, even if the producer is late or running an hour behind. You must be relaxed and cheerful even if the Casting Director has kept her head in the script from ten seconds after your entry. You must pretend it's a wonderful script even if you are gobsmacked that these wallies ever got the money to go ahead with the project.

So what do you do as you wait with a few paltry pages of script in your hands? If you are lucky you may also get a page summarising the story. Don't ignore this; it can give you valuable insights into your character, the style of the piece and, sometimes, the prejudice of the director. As you silently rehearse the piece in your mind don't get fixed on one interpretation. Think out three different ways to play the scene. You may not get a chance to try them but on your first read through you may feel an unreceptive frost coming across the table and you will be glad to suggest, "Of course it might be funnier to do it in Geordie – with a lisp."

I don't think it's a good idea to dress for the part. Producers usually like to think that they are adding something creative. So leave the Bank Manager's suit at home and keep the Tart's fishnet stockings for a party. However producers are not *that* creative so it's sensible to dress *towards* the part. Leave something to the imagination but don't make it an impossible challenge.

The interview will usually start with a little general chat, usually with your CV as the agenda – (so know what's on it)! Have a couple of "feelgood" stories to tell but be quick to notice when it's time to move on. If you have some questions on the production or the character ask them now, not as you walk out the door.

Don't flirt. This advice applies equally to men and women! The myth of the Casting Couch must have some basis in history but I haven't come across it. Casting is one of the most crucial stages of production and the fear of getting it wrong is a perfect bromide for the libido. Anyway, casting is rarely done singly and flirting with one person is likely to get right up the nose of the other. I've seen it happen.

When reading the scene try to get it right rather than fast; it's an audition not a performance; an indication of potential, not achievement. Make as much eye contact as possible. Eyes are all-important on television so you should also avoid any hairstyle that tends to hide them, even in a side-view.

When you have finished the scene don't be afraid to say, "Can I try that again?" Or "Can I try that standing-up?" This will usually open up a little conversation. Listen carefully to any suggestions made and be sure you understand them. Good directors will also be checking whether they can work well and communicate with you.

Finally, when the audition is clearly over, don't hang about. Don't start new and irrelevant conversations. The producers want you out of the room quickly so they can discuss you while you are fresh in their minds. Give them that chance or you could talk yourself out of a job!

Good Luck!'

Allan Foenander – well-known film and television Casting Director with several thousand commercials and numerous feature films and TVs to his credit, including *Shirley Valentine* for Paramount – directed by Lewis Gilbert, *The Most Dangerous Man in the World* for BBC – directed by Gavin Millar, *Great Expectations* for Disney – directed by Kevin Connor, UK casting for *The Night of the Fox* – directed by Charles Jarrott, *Heidi* for Disney – directed by Michael Rhodes, *The Old Curiosity Shop* for Disney – directed by Kevin Connor and most recently the UK casting for *Buffalo Girls* for CBS – directed by Rod Hardy:

'Make sure your agent finds out what the project is about and do some research on it. Check you are free for the shoot dates.

Make sure you know where the casting session is taking place and continue to turn up on time even when experience will teach you waiting around is nearly always part of the deal.

You will find some casting directors or their assistants run cattle markets rather than casting sessions. Turn up if you like that sort of thing. At least you may meet friends!

You will be called for many casting sessions and, if the casting is being done to an accurate brief, you will meet some of your lifelong competition. Sometimes you will be chosen, most times you will not. Don't be discouraged. View every casting session as an opportunity – you are being called, you are meeting new directors and producers.

If it's a commercial, don't joke about the project! The director and casting director may share your humour, but remember the product client is bound to be in love with the big profit brand name and the advertising agency producer, if they value their job, will pretend to be.

If it's a film or television, brief yourself on the book or subject if you can. Never assume all directors and producers have imagination! If the casting director requests you to dress for the part, work on it. Also work at the reputation of being a reliable, willing and pleasant character who is never too grand, if available, to take any part.'

Peter Aldersley – Radio Producer/Presenter for Radio Luxembourg, British Forces Network, BBC and Radio Stations in the USA:

'Radio is the most intimate of all media of communication. The microphone is the cruellest taskmaster for the actor (and all broadcasters) who has to rely solely on his voice to give a performance. It highlights the slightest flaw in speech, presentation and personality.

At a radio audition one looks for the quality of the voice required for the job and the actor's ability to produce the subtler nuances of delivery which would be lost in a theatre. For general broadcasting purposes the microphone technique could be described as speaking on a one to one basis.'

*

Valuable advice from 'auditioners' with many years of experience working in theatre, film, television and radio – and useful to look at the casting process from the opposite side of the table. 'Auditions are difficult for directors too.' Auditions and preparation for auditions are part of an actor's life. You are never too old and seldom too famous to be called to a casting session, and 'We'll let you know' is something you have to get used to. Why do we get ourselves so screwed up? 'The person most likely to get the job is the one that puts me at my ease.' There's no doubt about it, things seem to go much better when you are in a happy frame of mind and genuinely enjoy meeting a director or casting director. If you are harassed, have someting on your mind, or are simply trying to cram too many things into your day, an audition tends to go badly.

I remember two of my own auditions – both of them within a week of each other. The first was for a stage play. I was relaxed and easy. I had decided what to wear the night before, had borrowed the play from the library and knew more or less what I would be required to read. I was well prepared that day. I enjoyed meeting the director and her assistant and I got the part. My second audition was a disaster – a television interview at very short notice. I panicked, decided quite unnecessarily to get my hair done, had a row at home and arrived at my appointment in a thoroughly bad mood. The casting director was kind and very welcoming and the director was a nice friendly man who put me at my ease, but I was unable to relax and enjoy meeting them. I had too much cluttering up my mind and it showed. I didn't get the part.

Keep a clear head. Find out as much as you possibly can about the part you are auditioning for and what will be required of you. Make sure you leave plenty of time to get there – then relax. Most people are nice and want you to succeed. And above all – enjoy yourself!

AUDITION SPEECHES

American/Massachusetts
young/middle-aged

Blood Relations

Sharon Pollock

First performed at Theater 3, in Edmonton, Canada and at the
Canada House Cultural Centre, London in 1982. The play is set
in the time proper of 1902, with its 'dream thesis' set in 1892 at
Fall River, Massachusetts. It explores the events leading up to
the trial of Lizzie Borden, accused and acquitted of killing her
step-mother and father with an axe. In this scene the DEFENCE
LAWYER is addressing the jury.

Published in *Blood Relations and Other Plays* by Newest Publishers Limited,
Canada

Act 1

DEFENCE

Gentlemen of the Jury!! I ask you to look at the defendant, Miss Lizzie Borden. I ask you to recall the nature of the crime of which she is accused. I ask you – do you believe Miss Lizzie Borden, the youngest daughter of a scion of our community, a recipient of the fullest amenities our society can bestow upon its most fortunate members, do you believe Miss Lizzie Borden capable of wielding the murder weapon – thirty-two blows, gentlemen, thirty-two blows – fracturing Abigail Borden's skull, leaving her bloody and broken body in an upstairs bedroom, then, Miss Borden, with no hint of frenzy, hysteria, or trace of blood upon her person, engages in casual conversation with the maid, Bridget O'Sullivan, while awaiting her father's return home, upon which, after sending Bridget to her attic room, Miss Borden deals thirteen blows to the head of her father, and minutes later – in a state utterly compatible with that of a loving daughter upon discovery of murder most foul – Miss Borden calls for aid! Is this the aid we give her? Accusation of the most heinous and infamous of crimes? Do you believe Miss Lizzie Borden capable of these acts? I can tell you I do not!! I can tell you these acts of violence are acts of madness! Gentlemen! If this gentlewoman is capable of such an act – I say to you – look to your daughters – if this gentlewoman is capable of such an act, which of us can lie abed at night, hear a step upon the stairs, a rustle in the hall, a creak outside the door . . . Which of you can plump your pillow, nudge your wife, close your eyes, and sleep? Gentlemen, Lizzie Borden is not mad. Gentlemen, Lizzie Borden is not guilty.

South African/Cape Coloured
50s

Boesman and Lena

Athol Fugard

First performed at the Rhodes University Little Theatre and
directed by the author in 1969. BOESMAN is a Cape Coloured
man in his fifties, tramping the roads with his woman, Lena.
In this scene Lena and the Old Man are sitting huddled under
a blanket. BOESMAN stands in front of them with a bottle of
wine in his hand. He reminds Lena how they had watched the
'whiteman' bulldozing down the rotten shacks they were living
in, and forcing them to move on.

Published in *Selected Plays*, Athol Fugard, by Oxford University Press, Oxford

Act 2

BOESMAN
The lot of you! Crawling out of your holes. Like worms. *Babalas* as
the day you were born. That piece of ground was rotten with *dron-
kies*. Trying to save their rubbish, falling over each other . . . !
'Run you bastards! Whiteman's bulldozer is chasing you!'
(*Big laugh.*)

> [LENA And then he hit me for dropping the empties.]

BOESMAN (*the bulldozer*). Slowly it comes . . . slowly . . . big yellow
donner with its jawbone on the ground. One bite and there's a hole
in the earth! Whiteman on top. I watched him. He had to work, *ou
boeta*. Wasn't easy to tell that thing where to go. He had to work
with those knobs!
In reverse . . . take aim! . . . *maak sy bek oop!* . . . then horsepower
in top gear and smashed to hell. One push and it was flat. All of
them. Slum clearance! And what did we do? Stand and look . . .
The women and children sitting there with their snot and tears.

30

The *pondoks* falling. The men standing, looking, as the yellow *donner* pushed them over and then staring at the pieces when they were the only things left standing. I saw all that! The whiteman stopped the bulldozer and smoked a cigarette. I saw that too.

(*Another act.*)

'*Ek sê, my baas* . . . !' He threw me the *stompie*. '*Dankie, baas.*' . . . (*violently.*) Yes! *Dankie, baas.*

You should have said it too, sitting there with your sad story. Whiteman was doing us a favour. You should have helped him. He wasn't just burning *pondoks*. They alone can't stink like that. Or burn like that.

There was something else in that fire, something rotten. Us! Our sad stories, our smells, our world! And it burnt, *boeta*. It burnt. I watched that too.

The end was a pile of ashes. And quiet.

Then . . . 'Here!' . . . then I went back to the place where our *pondok* had been. It was gone! You understand that? Gone! I wanted to call you and show you. There where we crawled in and out like baboons, where we used to sit like them and eat, our head between our knees, our fingers in the pot, hiding away so that the others wouldn't see our food . . . I could stand there! There was room for me to stand straight. You know what that is? Listen now. I'm going to use a word. Freedom! *Ja*, I've heard them talk it. Freedom! That's what the whiteman gave us. I've got my feelings too, sister. It was a big one I had when I stood there. That's why I laughed, why I was happy. When we picked up our things and started to walk I wanted to sing. It was Freedom!

Babalas	slang for hung-over
dronkies	drunks
donner	bastard
ou boeta	old friend
maak sy bek oop	open its mouth
pondok	hut, shack
Ek sê, my baas	Hey, my boss
stompie	cigarette butt
Dankie, baas	Thank you boss/or master
Ja	yes

31

Liverpool
middle-aged

Breezeblock Park

Willy Russell

First presented at the Everyman Theatre, Liverpool in 1975 and
later at the Whitehall Theatre, London. The action takes place
at a family gathering over Christmas. On Christmas Eve Sandra
shocks her parents by announcing in front of everybody that
she is pregnant and is leaving home to live with her student
boyfriend, Tim. In this scene Sandra's father tries to talk to Tim
about the importance of marriage, while her uncle, TED, fires
general knowledge questions at him. Tim explains that Sandra
has found new interests in her life, things the family couldn't
possibly understand, like art, conversation and theatre. This
prompts TED to tell the story of how he once went to a theatre.

Published by Samuel French, London

Act 2

TED

Don't talk to me about theatres. I went to one once. 'Ey, John, what
was the name of that play, that play I took you an' y' mother to
see when it was rainin' in town? Remember?

[JOHN (*still absorbed in the television*) Waitin' for somethin' wasn't it?]

TED *Waitin' For Godot*. That was it. I'll tell y' about theatres. We went
in to see this thing, it was about these two tramps waitin' for this
mate of theirs. Well, I'm not kiddin' you? All this audience were
sittin' there waitin' for him as well. I could see straightaway what
was gonna happen though. I'd been in there about five minutes
an' I knew. I opened me programme didn't I, John? An' I looked
down the list, y'know where it gives the names of the characters
like? An' straightaway I knew, didn't I? His name's not there in
the programme y' see, this Godot's. Well, it's common sense, if his
name's not in the programme he's never gonna show up. Y' could
wait a hundred years an' he'd still never walk on to the bloody
stage. But all the rest of these stupid buggers in the place – they
didn't have the sense to look in the programme an' work it out for
themselves. I slipped out to this café next door an' read the paper.
I laughed meself silly at the rest of them next door. When our John
come out with his Mum, I said to him, didn't I, John? I said to him
– don't tell me – the Godot feller didn't turn up!
(*Pause*)

Translation from Russian
40s

The Cherry Orchard

Anton Chekhov
Translated by Elisaveta Fen

First performed at the Moscow Arts Theatre in 1904 and by the
Stage Society in England in 1911. The action of the play takes
place on the Estate of Mme Ranyevskaia, now up for auction to
pay for the family's debts.

A party is taking place in the drawing room and everyone is
waiting to hear news of the auction. LOPAKHIN, middle-aged
merchant and family friend, whose father and grandfather were
peasants, announces that he has bought the Estate, where he
used to run barefoot as a child. He has already been celebrating
before his arrival.

Published in *Plays*, by Penguin Books, London

Act 3

LOPAKHIN

Yes, I bought it. Wait a moment, ladies and gentlemen, do, please. I don't feel quite clear in my head, I hardly know how to talk . . . (*Laughs.*) When we got to the auction, Deriganov was there already. Of course, Leonid Andryeevich only had fifteen thousand roubles, and Deriganov at once bid thirty over and above the mortgage. I could see how things were going, so I muscled in and offered forty. He bid forty-five, I bid fifty-five; he kept on adding five thousand each time and I added ten thousand each time. Well, it finished at last – I bid ninety thousand over and above the mortgage, and I got the property. Yes, the cherry orchard's mine now! Mine! (*Laughs.*) My God! the cherry orchard's mine! Come on, tell me I'm drunk, tell me I'm out of my mind, say I've imagined all this . . . (*Stamps his foot.*) Don't laugh at me! If only my father and grandfather could rise from their graves and see everything that's happened . . . how their Yermolai, their much-beaten, half-literate Yermolai, the lad that used to run about with bare feet in the winter . . . how he's bought this estate, the most beautiful place on God's earth! Yes, I've bought the very estate where my father and grandfather were serfs, where they weren't even admitted to the kitchen! I must be asleep, I must be dreaming, I only think it's true . . . it's all just my imagination, my imagination's been wandering . . . (*Picks up the keys, smiling tenderly.*) She threw these down because she wanted to show she's not mistress here any more. (*Jingles the keys.*) Well, never mind. (*The band is heard tuning up.*) Hi! you musicians, come on now, play something, I want some music! Now then, all of you, just you wait and see Yermolai Lopakhin take an axe to the cherry orchard, just you see the trees come crashing down! We're going to build a whole lot of new villas, and our children and great-grandchildren are going to see a new living world growing up here . . . Come on there, let's have some music! . . . Come on, band, play up, play up! Everything must be just as I wish it now. (*Ironically.*) Here comes the new landowner, here comes the owner of the cherry orchard! (*He pushes a small table accidentally and nearly knocks over some candle-sticks.*) Never mind, I can pay for everything! (*Goes out with Pishchik.*)

English
middle-aged

The Country Wife

William Wycherley

First performed in 1675, probably at the Theatre Royal, Drury
Lane, London, by the King's Company. JACK PINCHWIFE, a
middle-aged rake, has married Margery, a pretty young country
girl, and is determined to keep her away from the young
'gallants' about town. When he discovers that the notorious
Master Horner has been paying attentions to her and has even
kissed her, he orders his young wife to sit down and write to
Horner telling him that she wants nothing more to do with him.
However, Margery is determined secretly to continue her
'romance'.

In this scene, PINCHWIFE enters to find Margery once more at
her writing desk. She tries to run out of the room, but he stops
her, snatches away the letter she has been writing and starts to
read it. It is a love letter to her 'Dear Master Horner...'

Published by A & C Black

Act 4, scene 4

PINCHWIFE

How's this! Nay, you shall not stir, madam. 'Dear, dear, dear Master Horner' – very well! – I have taught you to write letters to good purpose – but let's see't – 'First, I am to beg your pardon for my boldness in writing to you, which I'd have you to know I would not have done, had not you said first you loved me so extremely, which if you do, you will never suffer me to lie in the arms of another man, whom I loathe, nauseate, and detest' – Now you can write these filthy words! But what follows? – 'Therefore I hope you will speedily find some way to free me from this unfortunate match, which was never, I assure you, of my choice, but I'm afraid 'tis already too far gone. However, if you love me, as I do you, you will try what you can do, but you must help me away before tomorrow, or else, alas, I shall be for ever out of your reach, for I can defer no longer our' – (*The letter concludes*) 'Our'? What is to follow 'our'? Speak, what? Our journey into the country I suppose? Oh, woman, damned woman! And love, damned love, their old tempter! For this is one of his miracles. In a moment he can make those blind that could see, and those see that were blind, those dumb that could speak, and those prattle who were dumb before; nay, what is more than all, make these dough-baked, senseless, indocile animals, women, too hard for us, their politic lords and rulers, in a moment. But make an end of your letter and then I'll make an end of you thus, and all my plagues together. (*Draws his sword*)

match	This usually means an engagement rather than a marriage; seems a bit disingenuous.
dough-baked	half-baked
indocile	hard to teach
politic	lawful

Italian
young

Cymbeline

William Shakespeare

Probably first produced in 1610. Imogen, daughter of Cymbeline, King of Britain, secretly marries Posthumus Leonatus. When her father discovers the marriage, Posthumus is banished. He flees to Rome, and there he meets the crafty IACHIMO and foolishly makes a wager with him that nobody could seduce his virtuous wife, Imogen. IACHIMO, determined to win the wager, comes to Britain, but is unable to ingratiate himself into Imogen's favour. He hides himself in a chest in her bedchamber, so that he can note down every detail of the room, and even steals the bracelet from her wrist while she is asleep, in order to be able to convince Posthumus that he has seduced her.

Act 2, scene 2

IACHIMO

> The crickets sing, and man's o'er-labour'd sense
> Repairs itself by rest. Our Tarquin thus
> Did softly press the rushes ere he waken'd
> The chastity he wounded. Cytherea,
> How bravely thou becom'st they bed! fresh lily,
> And whiter than the sheets! That I might touch!
> But kiss; one kiss! Rubies unparagon'd,
> How dearly they do't! 'Tis her breathing that
> Perfumes the chamber thus. The flame o' th' taper
> Bows toward her and would under-peep her lids
> To see th' enclosed lights, now canopied
> Under these windows white and azure, lac'd
> With blue of heaven's own tinct. But my design
> To note the chamber. I will write all down:
> Such and such pictures; there the window; such
> Th' adornment of her bed; the arras, figures –
> Why, such and such; and the contents o' th' story.
> Ah, but some natural notes about her body
> Above ten thousand meaner movables
> Would testify, t' enrich mine inventory.
> O sleep, thou ape of death, lie dull upon her!
> And be her sense but as a monument,
> Thus in a chapel lying! Come off, come off;
> (*Taking off her bracelet.*)

Set in Venice
middle-aged/elderly

Daughters of Venice

Don Taylor

First produced by the Chiswick Youth Theatre at the Water-
man's Arts Centre in 1991 and then professionally by the
Quercus Theatre company at the Wilde Theatre in 1993, it is set
in eighteenth century Venice. The 'Daughters' of the title are
the young orphans taken in and cared for by the Sisters of the
Pietà. In this scene, the famous composer, VIVALDI, now
middle-aged to elderly, urges Anna Maria, orphan and brilliant
musician, to forget her ambitions to become an opera singer.

Published by Samuel French, London

Act 2

VIVALDI

Listen child! . . . You know nothing, you have lived your life in a convent, and you have no understanding of the world, or what a singer's life is like, what any artist's life is like! It isn't only making beautiful sounds. It's having the right aristocratic protector, who will guard you with his paid assassins, from other aristocratic gentlemen, and keep you in his palace for his private use when you are not in the Opera House. It means repaying his favours with your own, in whatever way he asks. It means keeping at least two others in the background, unknown to the first, who are just as mad to get you on to their stages and into their beds, so that when the first drops you, as he will, you are not left naked in the street. It's being kidnapped at the stage door because some Cardinal has taken a fancy to you, and Princes of the Church must have their way, even over noblemen sometimes. It means working too hard, and singing too often, bullying composers to write you showy enough arias so that your reputation doesn't slide. It means losing your voice at fifty and your looks at thirty-five, and dying in poverty in a gutter somewhere, starved, ill or murdered. It's spending your whole life thinking of money, power and reputation, and whose property you are this week, just to ensure that when the moment comes, you can open your mouth and practise your art, and do what you were born to do. An artist lives for money, fame, reputation and power, because without those things he cannot practise his art, and that is all that matters to him, more than house, home, pleasure, more even than life. I am a composing machine, that's all. I became a priest, because it was the only way a poor boy could get an education, but I never say Mass, and have not done for twenty years, because I have no time for anything but music. I have a mania for it, a consuming power that I can't control. I compose like a madman, like a wheatfield swept by the wind of God, or a forest on fire, I can do nothing else. Sometimes it is good, sometimes less good, sometimes so bad it makes me weep for having written it, but I can't stop the fire burning, and everything in my life, everything, comes second to that flame. You can't do that. You can't live like that. All opera singers are monsters, because they have to be if they are to practise their art to the best of their ability. You are not a monster. Go to a convent and live in peace.

Edinburgh
24

Dead Dad Dog

John McKay

First performed at the Traverse Theatre, Edinburgh in May, 1988 and later that year at the Royal Court Theatre Upstairs, London. ECK is twenty-four and described as an aspiring Scottish media type, currently unemployed. Throughout the action he is dogged by the ghost of his dead Dad – a comic nightmare. In this opening scene, ECK has just come down to breakfast and is anticipating the successful outcome of his interview that morning with BBC Scotland. His soliloquy is interrupted by the appearance of Willie his 'Dead Dad'.

Published in *Scot-Free* New Scottish Plays, by Nick Hern Books, London

Scene 1

ECK
Today. Hm. A wee bit dull.
No matter. Hello birds. Hello back green. Hello pink tee-shirt on somebody's line.
Today.
Today's gonna be a good one. An I'll tell you why.
Number one. I've got up. Thank you, God.
Number two. After watchin most of my friends scurry south to weather the long winter of recession and repression, my efforts to hang on in the country where the action's at but the cash is not have finally been rewarded. That is, this morning I've landed an interview for a halfway decent job. At 10.30 a.m. BBC Scotland will be exposed to the irresistible charm and dynamic ideas of hotshot Alexander Dundee. By 10.45 I'll have ma own series.
(*Confidential.*)
Yesterday I got a card from ma pal Donald. Just started workin for a trendy newspaper in London. Says they're lookin for another writer. Says I should apply. Well I say ha ha no sell out.
Number three. M-hm, number three, tonight I'm meeting Roseanne. So if you hear a sound like a pneumatic drill, it's no Embra Corporation digging up the roads again – it's my heart saying to my brain, wise up greystuff, this girl makes me wanna play the bongos. Wah!
(*Watch.*)
9.15. Time enough to have some breakfast. But on a day like this, it's no just breakfast. It's hello cornflakes in yer bright square box, what a nice free gift you gave me last week, out you come, dinnae mind ma hand, and then hello milk chock full of calcium yum yum sploosh.
He bends over and listens to the bowl.
No sound. Wrong brand. No matter. You're fresh and you're crunchy and today you are mine, you are indeed my . . .
Willie has appeared. Eck drops the bowl of cornflakes.

[WILLIE Hello son.]

ECK Dad.

American/New York
34

Death of a Salesman

Arthur Miller

First produced in New York in 1949 and later that year at the
Phoenix Theatre in London. The action takes place in the house
of the salesman, Willy Loman, and the places he visits in New
York and Boston in the late 1940s. BIFF, aged 34, is Willy's elder
son, a dreamer who is unable to settle in any job for long. He
has returned home after a year's absence and is talking to his
younger brother, Happy, in the bedroom they used to share as
children.

Published by Penguin Books, London

Act 1

BIFF
I tell ya, Hap, I don't know what the future is. I don't know – what
I'm supposed to want.

   [HAPPY What do you mean?]

BIFF Well, I spent six or seven years after high school trying to
work myself up. Shipping clerk, salesman, business of one kind or
another. And it's a measly manner of existence. To get on that
subway on the hot mornings in summer. To devote your whole life
to keeping stock, or making phone calls, or selling or buying. To
suffer fifty weeks of the year for the sake of a two-week vacation,
when all you really desire is to be outdoors, with your shirt off.
And always to have to get ahead of the next fella. And still – that's
how you build a future.

   [HAPPY Well, you really enjoy it on a farm? Are you content out there?]

BIFF (*with rising agitation*) Hap, I've had twenty or thirty different

44

kinds of job since I left home before the war, and it always turns out the same. I just realized it lately. In Nebraska when I herded cattle, and the Dakotas, and Arizona, and now in Texas. It's why I came home now, I guess, because I realized it. This farm I work on, it's spring there now, see? And they've got about fifteen new colts. There's nothing more inspiring or – beautiful than the sight of a mare and a new colt. And it's cool there now, see? Texas is cool now, and it's spring. And whenever spring comes to where I am, I suddenly get the feeling, my God, I'm not gettin' anywhere! What the hell am I doing, playing around with horses, twenty-eight dollars a week! I'm thirty-four years old, I oughta be makin' my future. That's when I come running home. And now, I get here, and I don't know what to do with myself. (*After a pause.*) I've always made a point of not wasting my life, and everytime I come back here I know that all I've done is to waste my life.

[HAPPY You're a poet, you know that, Biff? You're a – you're an idealist!]

BIFF No, I'm mixed up very bad. Maybe I oughta get married. Maybe I oughta get stuck into something. Maybe that's my trouble. I'm like a boy. I'm not married, I'm not in business, I just – I'm like a boy. Are you content, Hap? You're a success, aren't you? Are you content?

New York
63

Death of a Salesman

Arthur Miller

First performed in England at the Phoenix Theatre in 1949, the play is set in WILLY LOMAN's house and the various places he visits in New York and Boston in the late forties. WILLY has worked as a salesman for the Wagner Company for thirty-four years, but now, at the age of sixty-three, they have taken away his salary and he is expected to work on commission only, driving long distances and often returning home having earnt nothing at all. He is exhausted – a man at the end of his tether. In this scene he approaches Howard, the son of his old boss, and reminds him that he had promised to find him a position in town, where he won't have to travel anymore. Howard tells him there is no place for him except on the road.

Published by Heinemann Educational, Oxford

Act 2

WILLY (*angrily*)
Business is definitely business, but just listen for a minute. You don't understand this. When I was a boy – eighteen, nineteen – I was already on the road. And there was a question in my mind as to whether selling had a future for me. Because in those days I had a yearning to go to Alaska. See, there were three gold strikes in one month in Alaska, and I felt like going out. Just for the ride, you might say.

[HOWARD (*barely interested*) Don't say.]

WILLY Oh, yeah, my father lived many years in Alaska. He was an adventurous man. We've got quite a little streak of self-reliance in our family. I thought I'd go out with my older brother and try to locate him and maybe settle in the North with the old man. And I was almost decided to go, when I met a salesman in the Parker House. His name was Dave Singleman. And he was eighty-four years old, and he'd drummed merchandise in thirty-one states. And old Dave, he'd go up to his room, y'understand, put on his green velvet slippers – I'll never forget – and pick up his phone and call the buyers, and without ever leaving his room, at the age of eighty-four, he made his living. And when I saw that, I realized that selling was the greatest career a man could want. 'Cause what could be more satisfying than to be able to go, at the age of eighty-four, into twenty or thirty different cities, and pick up a phone, and be remembered and loved and helped by so many different people? Do you know? when he died – and by the way, he died the death of a salesman, in his green velvet slippers in the smoker of the New York, New Haven, and Hartford, going into Boston – when he died, hundreds of salesmen and buyers were at his funeral. Things were sad on a lotta trains for months after that. (*He stands up. Howard has not looked at him.*) In those days there was personality in it, Howard. There was respect, and comradeship, and gratitude in it. Today, it's all cut and dried, and there's no chance for bringing friendship to bear – or personality. You see what I mean? They don't know me any more.

American/New Hampshire
young

The Devil's Disciple

George Bernard Shaw

First seen in New York in 1897 and produced in London at the Savoy Theatre in 1907, it is set in the town of Westerbridge, New Hampshire in the year 1777, when the American colonies were fighting for independence. RICHARD (DICK) is the sardonic eldest son of the Dudgeons and detested by many for his irreligious attitudes and the shame he has brought upon the family. He is self-styled 'the devil's disciple' because as a child he prayed to the devil and promised him his soul, so that his spirit wouldn't be broken by the strict puritanism he was forced to endure. However, when the English soldiers occupy the town and orders are given to hang the Presbyterian Minister, Anthony Anderson, DICK gallantly takes his place. At the gallows the chaplain asks DICK to control himself and submit to the divine will.

Published in *Three Plays for Puritans*, by Penguin Books, London

Act 3

RICHARD

Answer for your own will, sir, and those of your accomplices here (*indicating Burgoyne and Swindon*): I see little divinity about them or you. You talk to me of Christianity when you are in the act of hanging your enemies. Was there ever such blasphemous non-sense! (*To Swindon, more rudely*) Youve got up the solemnity of the occasion, as you call it, to impress the people with your own dignity – Handel's music and a clergyman to make murder look like piety! Do you suppose *I* am going to help you? Youve asked me to choose the rope because you dont know your own trade well enough to shoot me properly. Well, hang away and have done with it . . . (*with the horror of death upon him*) Do you think this is a pleasant sort of thing to be kept waiting for? Youve made up your mind to commit murder: well, do it and have done with it . . . Hark ye, General Burgoyne. If you think that I like being hanged, youre mistaken. I dont like it; and I dont mean to pretend that I do. And if you think I'm obliged to you for hanging me in a gentlemanly way, youre wrong there too. I take the whole business in devilish bad part; and the only satisfaction I have in it is that youll feel a good deal meaner than I'll look when it's over. (*He turns away, and is striding to the cart when Judith advances and interposes with her arms stretched out to him. Richard, feeling that a very little will upset his self-possession, shrinks from her, crying*) What are you doing here? This is no place for you. (*She makes a gesture as if to touch him. He recoils impatiently*) No: go away, go away; youll unnerve me. Take her away, will you . . . (*imploringly to those around him, and finally to Burgoyne, as the least stolid of them*) Take her away. Do you think I want a woman near me now? . . . (*in the strong voice of a man who has conquered the bitterness of death*) Your watch is two minutes slow by the town clock, which I can see from here, General. (*The town clock strikes the first stroke of twelve. Involuntarily the people flinch at the sound, and a subdued groan breaks from them*) Amen! my life for the world's future!

American/New England
young

Diff'rent

Eugene O'Neill

First produced in New York in 1920, it is set in the parlour of the Crosby home, in a seaport village in New England, covering a period between 1890 and 1920. CALEB WILLIAMS, a sea captain just returned from a long sea voyage, is planning to marry his childhood sweetheart, Emma, in two days time. However, Emma has found out that he spent a night alone on board his ship with a naked South Sea Island girl, and demands an explanation.

Published in *The Collected Plays of Eugene O'Neill*, by Jonathan Cape, London

Act 1

CALEB (*after a long pause – regretfully*)
Waal, I guess what he told is true enough.

[EMMA (*wounded*). Oh!]

CALEB But that ain't no good reason for tellin' it. Them sort o' things ought to be kept among men. (*After a pause – gropingly.*) I didn't want nothin' like that to happen, Emmer. I didn't mean it to. I was thinkin' o' how you might feel – even down there. That's why I stayed aboard all the time when the boys was ashore. I wouldn't have b'lieved it could happen – not to me. (*A pause.*) I wish you could see them islands, Emmer, and be there for a time. Then you might see – It's hard's hell to explain, and you havin' never seen 'em. Everything is diff'rent down there – the weather, and the trees and water. You git lookin' at it all, and you git to feel diff'rent from what you do at home here. It's purty hereabouts sometimes – like now, in spring – but it's purty there all the time – and down there you notice it and you git feelin' – diff'rent. And them native women – they're diff'rent. A man don't think of 'em as women – like you. But they're purty – in their fashion – and at night they sings – and it's all diff'rent like something you'd see in a painted picture. (*A pause.*) That night when she swum out and got aboard when I was alone, she caught me by s'prise. I wasn't expectin' nothin' o' that sort. I tried to make her git back to land at fust – but she wouldn't go. She couldn't understand enough English for me to tell her how I felt – and I reckon she wouldn't have seed my p'int anyhow, her bein' a native. (*A pause.*) And then I was afeerd she'd catch cold goin' round all naked and wet in the moonlight – though it was warm – and I wanted to wrap a blanket round her. (*He stops as if he had finished.*)

[EMMA (*after a long, tense pause – dully*) Then you own up – there really was something happened?]

CALEB (*after a pause*) I was sorry for it, after. I locked myself in the cabin and left her to sleep out on deck.

Translated from Norwegian
middle-aged

A Doll's House

Henrik Ibsen
Translated by Peter Watts

First performed in 1879 at the Theatre Royal, Copenhagen and in England at the Novelty Theatre in 1889. The action takes place in Helmer's apartment near a market town in southern Norway, over Christmas. TORVALD HELMER, a middle-aged lawyer has recently been made Manager of the Savings Bank. He discovers that his wife Nora forged her father's signature in order to obtain money to send TORVALD away when he was ill. Now she is being threatened with exposure by the vindictive Krogstad, an employee at the bank who has just been dismissed and is determined to use any means to get his job back. In this scene TORVALD accuses Nora of having no sense of morals and being unfit to bring up their children.

Published in *Plays* vol. 2, by Penguin Books, London

Act 3

HELMER

I might have known that something of this sort would happen – I should have foreseen it. All your father's shiftless character – Be quiet! – all your father's shiftless character has come out in you. No religion, no morality, no sense of duty . . . So this is what I get for condoning his fault! I did it for your sake, and this is how you repay me! . . . You've completely wrecked my happiness, you've ruined my whole future! Oh, it doesn't bear thinking of. I'm in the power of a man without scruples; he can do what he likes with me – ask what he wants of me – order me about as he pleases, and I dare not refuse. And I'm brought so pitifully low all because of a shiftless woman! . . . No rhetoric, please! Your father was always ready with fine phrases too. How would it help me if you were 'out of the way', as you call it? Not in the least! He can still see that the thing gets about, and once he does, I may very well be suspected of having been involved in your crooked dealings. They may well think that I was behind it – that I put you up to it. And it's you that I have to thank for all this – and after I've cherished you all through our married life. *Now* do you realize what you've done to me? . . . It's so incredible that I can't grasp it. But we must try to come to some understanding. Take off that shawl – take it off, I tell you. Somehow or other I must try to appease him – the thing must be hushed up at all costs. As for ourselves – we must seem to go on just as before . . . but only in the eyes of the world of course. You will remain here in my house – that goes without saying – but I shall not allow you to bring up the children . . . I shouldn't dare trust you with them. Oh, to think that I should have to say this to someone I've loved so much – someone I still . . . Well, that's all over – it must be; from now on, there'll be no question of happiness, but only of saving the ruin of it – the fragments – the mere façade . . .

(*There is a ring at the front door.*)

(*collecting himself*): What's that – at this hour? Can the worst have – Could he . . . ? Keep out of sight, Nora – say that you're ill.

Jamaican
young

An Echo in the Bone

Dennis Scott

First presented by the University Drama Society at the Creative
Arts Centre, Jamaica in 1974. It is set during a traditional Nine
Night Ceremony held to honour the spirit of the dead. Although
the main action takes place in the present, the play flashes back
to the time of plantations and slavery. In this sequence, set
in 1831, the character, DREAMBOAT, re-enacts a scene in an
auctioneer's office, where he is selling slaves for his master.

Published in *Plays for Today*, by Longman, Essex

Act 1

DREAM

Now sir, to business. The females, you will wonder what the other does here. Now the master, Lord bless him, he's prepared a fine surprise for you sir – this one fell into his hands from Barbados, a gentleman going home and had to sell out everything and here we come upon – but I shan't tell you, you shall judge for yourself. But these – ah. (*Sighs with pleasure. Hands Rattler a blank sheet, ink and pen*) Sisters. Hardly more than nineteen, no bad habits yet. Now let me see. (*Consults a paper*) You want one for breeding, one for er, a houseworker. Of course. Nervous you see, but that's always a good sign, like a good hunter, the master says, don't you agree sir? Now my pretties, stand steady, this is your lucky day. Show your best side. A fine problem, sir indeed I hardly know how to advise you. Now this – (*To Brigit*) please make note, the wide hips, the breasts just fulling out. Teeth of course . . . docile. No offspring yet. Do you wish to see proof of virginity – or perhaps you'll wish to see for yourself – indeed, that's hardly necessary, we have a long association of trust, don't we, sir. Calves, well muscled, exceedingly well turned, you will notice. Now, now! Stand quiet, no harm will come to you! Ah. I remember the day of my selling, just a small boy, and so frightened. There was such a lot to learn. But my master, oh, a wiser gentleman you couldn't find . . . such a lot he thought of me! Ah yes. Notice how he holds the pen, sir. Ah, a fine surprise when he finishes.
Of course, slowly, my beauties.
(*The girls are sobbing a little.*) Come, come! The other . . . Here is the doctor's certificate, equally untouched. Notice the nipples. Fire in this one sir, you'll forgive my saying so. But the clear eyes show how easily she can be taught. All kinds of things.
(*Stone goes to Lally. Puts on a glove. Feels her shape, presses on her jaws to make them open. Runs his hands up between her legs. She gasps and tenses. Considers her head on one side.*)
That's enough. (*Takes paper from Rattler who stands stiffly with the ink and pen in two hands*) Now sir, we in the business know how difficult it is to find a good reckoner. This one falls into your lap. He can read, write and reckon like a schoolmaster. The master thinks to give you proof and turn your head with good luck, no hesitation. This is what he has been writing while we spoke here, sir.

Jamaican
25

An Echo in the Bone

Dennis Scott

First presented by the University Drama Society at the Creative
Arts Centre, Jamaica in 1974. It is set during a traditional Nine
Night Ceremony held to honour the spirit of the dead. The main
action takes place in the present, but in this scene SONSON,
aged twenty-five, takes over the spirit or persona of his dead
father, Crew and re-enacts the scene which led to his death.

Published in *Plays For Today*, by Longman, Essex

Act 2

SONSON

Leave here? I can't do that! How I will live? My navel string bury
here, woman. Give up the land? You don't want me to do that?
. . . I know every step of it. Every bush; like the back of me hand.
Is a history behind every foot of it. Look at me, woman! I don't
have nothing except what I get from the ground. I born by it and
marry by it and one day it going to kill me. Maybe even now, but
is what I know, it is what nothing can change. I trying to tell you,
and I don't have the word to tell you, I am like a dumb man trying
to tell you what happen to him. I only can trace the line here in
the hard dirt, see? And the line going from here to there, and this
end is where them bring my great grandfather, here, and this is
me. If you take away the line from the ground I am nothing. I am
nobody! . . . The land is everything! Everything! I will tell you! My
father and his father sweat for it; year after year. It is my birthright
that say I am not a slave anymore. I don't have to work for no man,
I don't have to beg no man for bread to pass down to my children.
And my woman don't have to go slave in any whiteman house, I
don't care how much they pay you! Rachel me love, don't take that

away from me. I will find a way out. Trust me. (*Pause*) Mass Charles. I going to talk to him . . . Don't him born here? Grow up here same as me and him. Him is a white man yes, but he know how a man like me feel about the land, and him will listen. The river rise on his land, and when the landfall turn it from the property, it still flowing through the estate. Mass Charlie have water, and to spare. I will work out something with him. You will see. Wife, go take off you good clothes and wait for me. I will be back before dark . . . I don't have nothing to be ashamed of. This how a man look when he work for his living. I is a cultivator, I look like one and I smell like one. Is a honest thing, and I don't have no need to hide it, even if is only begging I going to do. Lawd, sun beating like a drum on me head . . .

[RACHEL Crew, walk good.]

SONSON Go on now.

(*Rachel moves away from him. He brushes off his trousers, stacks the machete in his belt, empties the flask, wipes his mouth on his hand, throws the bottle away. Waves her off grinning. She backs away, then turns and goes quickly. He blinks up at the sky.*)

Hold on, father. Is a long walk I making, so cool off little bit, eeh? (*Exits*)

German
22

Five Finger Exercise

Peter Shaffer

First produced at the Comedy Theatre, London in 1958 and set in a weekend cottage, in the English countryside. WALTER LANGER is a young German employed by Mrs Harrington as tutor to her teenage daughter. He has always pretended to the Harringtons that his parents are dead, but now he confesses to their son, Clive, that they are both alive and that his father was a Nazi Officer.

Published in *Three Plays*, Peter Shaffer, by Penguin Books, London

Act 2, scene 1

WALTER

What can you see? My parents? My father – can you see him, in his Nazi uniform? . . . (*crosses to back of armchair*) Oh, yes. He was a great man in the town. Everybody was afraid of him, so was I . . . When war broke out he went off to fight and we did not see him for almost six years. When he came back, he was still a Nazi. Everybody else was saying, 'We never liked them. We never supported them.' But not him! 'I've supported them,' he said. 'Hitler was the greatest man our country has seen since Bismarck. Even now we are defeated, we are the greatest country in Europe. And one day we will win, because we have to win . . .' (*He crosses and sits in the chair right of dining-table.*) Every night he used to make me recite the old slogans against Jews and Catholics and the Liberals. When I forgot, he would hit me – so many mistakes, so many hits.

[CLIVE But your mother?]

WALTER My mother . . . she worshipped him. Even after we found out.

[CLIVE What?]

WALTER That during the war . . . he worked at Auschwitz concentration camp . . . He was one of their most efficient officers. (*A slight pause.*) Once he told me how many . . . (*He stops in distress. His voice was dead with loathing.*) I could have killed him. I could have killed him till he was dead. And she worshipped him – my mother. She used to smile at him, stare at him – as though he owned her. And when he used to hit me, she would just – just look away as though what he was doing was difficult, yes – but unavoidable, like training a puppy. That was my mother.

[CLIVE I'm sorry.]

WALTER (*recovering*) So you see, Clive, I do know what it is like to have a family. And what I look for is somewhere . . . where now and then good spirits can sit on the roof.

Translated from Norwegian
young

Ghosts

Henrik Ibsen
Translated by Peter Watts

Written in 1891, *Ghosts* caused an uproar and none of the European theatres would stage it. Its first production was given by a Chicago touring company and it was staged in London in 1914. It is set in a large garden-room in the widowed Mrs Alving's country house, overlooking a gloomy fjord, half-hidden by continual rain. Her young son OSVALD has returned home and a monument to his father is due to be consecrated. The house is full of ghosts of the past and OSVALD tells his mother that he is suffering from a fatal disease (which will eventually destroy his brain).

Published in *Ghosts and Other Plays*, by Penguin Books, London

Act 2

OSVALD

It was directly after the last time I was home. I'd just got back to Paris, when I began to get the most violent headaches – they seemed to be mostly at the back of my head. It was as if a ring of iron, from my neck upwards, were being screwed tight . . .
At first I thought they were only the ordinary headaches that I used to get so badly when I was small . . .
But they weren't – I soon realized that. I couldn't work any longer. I wanted to start on a big new picture, but it was as if my skill had failed me – all my powers were paralysed, I couldn't collect my thoughts, my head seemed to swim and everything spun round. Oh, it was terrible. At last I sent for the doctor – and I learned the truth from him . . .
He was one of the best doctors there. I had to tell him just how I

felt, and then he began to ask me a whole lot of questions that didn't seem to me to have anything to do with it. I couldn't see what the man was driving at . . . –

At last he said: 'You have been more or less riddled from your birth.' The actual word he used was *'vermoulu'* . . .

I didn't understand either, and I asked him to explain. Then the old cynic said – (*He clenches his fists.*) Oh . . . ! –

He said, 'The sins of the fathers are visited on the children . . .' – I nearly hit him in the face . . .

(*smiling sadly*) Yes, what do you think of that? Of course I assured him that anything like that was quite impossible. But do you think he'd give way? No, he stood firm, and it was only when I produced your letters and translated all the bits about Father for him . . . –

Well then, of course, he had to admit that he was on the wrong track. That was when I learned the truth – the incredible truth: I ought never to have joined in that gloriously happy life with my friends; it's been too much for my strength. It's all been my own fault! . . .

According to him, there was no other possible explanation. *That's* what's so terrible: my whole life ruined – irreparably ruined – and all through my own thoughtlessness. All the things I meant to do in the world . . . I daren't think about them again – I *can't* think about them. Oh, if only I could start afresh and make my life over again . . .

If only it *had* been something I'd inherited – something I wasn't to blame for . . . But this! It's so shameful to have thrown away my health and happiness – everything in the world – so thoughtlessly, so recklessly . . . My future – my life itself!

Yorkshire
20s to late 70s

Happy Jack

John Godber

First presented professionally by the Hull Truck Company in 1985 and set in Yorkshire. The actors speak directly to the audience and re-enact incidents in the lives of JACK, a colliery worker and his wife, Liz, starting with them both in their late seventies and moving backwards in time to when they first started going out together. In this scene, JACK, now middle-aged, is talking to his young grandson about his schooldays, and advising him to make something of himself and not end up 'a bloody miner'.

Published in *John Godber Five Plays*, by Penguin Books, London

Act 2

JACK

Ar, once or twice, it's rate an' all is that bugger. I never put much store by book learning, didn't seem to make much sense to me. I've got two hands, and I can handle a shovel, and I know how coal gets made. That's about the sum total of my schooling. Mind you, I can print really well. That's all I can remember from school, having to print out letters all the bloody time. I've learnt this much: if you want owt, you've got to work for it, nobody's gonna hand it to yer on a plate. I've worked for everything we've got . . . and that's not much by other standards. Before Liz had our Ian I never had a day off from the pit . . . never had a laker . . . I thought I was working for sommat, sommat important. Huh? I must have been bloody loose. We wa' scratin' and saving up trying to mek sommat for ussens. I never had time to see that I wa' getting older, slowing down. I'd been doing the same amount of work at forty as I was doing at twenty . . . ar . . . working? Working for what? For who? National Coal Board. (*Laughs.*) I've upset some people in my time, lad, I've upset some of the buggers.
(*A beat.*)
Don't thee be like thee grandfather. Thee go and mek sommat of thee life. Don't thee be a bloody miner. For God's sake, make sommat for yersen.
(*Blackout.*).

laker   a day off

65

White South African
late 20s

Hello and Goodbye

Athol Fugard

First produced at the Library Theatre, Johannesburg in 1965.
JOHNNIE SMIT, a poor white Afrikaner, has been living with his
crippled father in a cramped cottage in Port Elizabeth until the
old man's recent death. His sister, Hester, having heard her
father was likely to die, returns home looking for a share of his
disability compensation. JOHNNIE pretends that his father is still
alive and lying in bed in the next room. Together they search
through boxes and suitcases looking for the money. Old memories flood back and JOHNNIE reminds Hester how 'Daddy' was
always telling them about The Bad Years.

Published in *Selected Plays*, by Oxford University Press, Oxford

Act 2

JOHNNIE

1931, or '30 or '32. Don't you remember? The Bad Years. 1931 onwards. When he worked on the line to Graaff-Reinet. You remember, man. Daddy. He was always telling us. Something terrible had happened somewhere and it was Bad Times . . . no jobs, no money. That's what he dreams about now.

The kaffirs sit and watch them work. The white men are hungry. Everybody is greedy. Specially about work – more greedy even than with food. Because work is food – not just today but tomorrow is work. So men look at another man's work the way they used to look at his wife. And those that got it work until the blisters burst and their backs break. He queued for a week to get the job – laying sleepers. Last week ten of his friends was fired. So you work like devils. *They got to see you work!*

And all the time the kaffirs sit and watch the white man doing kaffir work – hungry for the work. They are dying by the dozen!

And then one day in the kloof the other side of Heuningvlei he thought the end had come. His back was hurting like never before, his blisters were running blood. So he cried in the wilderness. 'Why hast thou forsaken me, Lord?' Like Moses. 'Why hast thou forsaken thy lamb?' But it wasn't the end.

That night the railway doctor came to the tents with embrocation and bandages – and he carried on. One mile a day. Heuningvlei, Boesmanspoort, Tierberg, Potterstop . . . He knows them all! And when they reached Graaff-Reinet the Lord's purpose in all suffering was revealed. Because there he met Mommie.

'I was there in the wilderness – like Moses. The sleepers bent my back, the Lord bent my spirit. But I was not broken. It took dynamite to do that!' Hey?

Lancashire
60s

Hindle Wakes

Stanley Houghton

First produced at the Aldwych Theatre, London in 1912, it is about Lancashire people in Hindle, a small manufacturing town. NATHANIEL JEFFCOTE is a gaunt, domineering man of about sixty and the owner of Daisy Bank Mill, who started life in a weaving shed. Money means power, and he is determined that one day his son, Alan, will be the richest man in Hindle. In this scene he finds out that Alan, who is engaged to Beatrice, daughter of the eminent Sir Timothy Farrer, has spent the weekend with Fanny Hawthorn, one of his own weavers. He insists that Alan breaks off his engagement to Beatrice and does the 'right thing' by Fanny.

Published by Sidgwick & Jackson, London

Act 1, scene 3

JEFFCOTE

So thou thinks it easy for me to see thee wed Fanny Hawthorn? Hearken! Dost know how I began life? Dost know that I started as tenter in Walmesley's shed when I were eight years of age, and that when the time comes I shall leave the biggest fortune ever made in the cotton trade in Hindle? Dost know what my thought has been when labouring these thirty years to get all that brass together? Not what pleasure I could get out of spending, but what power and influence I were piling up the while. I was set on founding a great firm that would be famous not only all over Lancashire but all over the world, like Horrockses or Calverts or Hornbys of Blackburn. Dost think as I weren't right glad when thou goes and gets engaged to Tim Farrar's lass? Tim Farrar as were Mayor of Hindle and got knighted when the King come to open the new Town Hall. Tim Farrar that owns Lane End Shed, next biggest place to Daisy Bank in Hindle. Why, it were the dearest wish of my heart to see thee wed Tim Farrar's lass; and, happen, to see thee running both mills afore I died. And now what falls out? Lad as I'd looked to to keep on the tradition and build the business bigger still, goes and weds one of my own weavers! Dost think that's no disappointment to me? Hearken! I'd put down ten thousand quid if thou could honestly wed Beatrice Farrar. But thou can't honestly wed her, not if I put down a million. There's only one lass thou can honestly wed now, and that's Fanny Hawthorn, and by God I'm going to see that thou does it!

(*Jeffcote stalks out of the room with his candle and his poker, which he has never put down, and Alan remains huddled up and motionless in a corner of the arm-chair.*)

Set in ancient Greece
young

Hippolytus

Euripides
Translated by Philip Vellacott

Written in 428 BC and set in front of the Palace at Trozen, where King Theseus is spending a year of voluntary exile with Phaedra, his young wife. Phaedra has fallen hopelessly in love with her stepson, HIPPOLYTUS. Lying on her sick bed and near to death, she confesses her shameful secret to her old Nurse, who in turn confides in HIPPOLYTUS, inferring that there is only one way to save her mistress. HIPPOLYTUS, outraged by her suggestions, and overheard by Phaedra, berates all women and the servants who 'traffic their lewdness'.

Published in *Euripides Three Plays*, by Penguin Books, London

HIPPOLYTUS
    O Zeus! Why have you established in the sunlit world
    This counterfeit coin, woman, to curse the human race?
    If you desired to plant a mortal stock, why must
    The means for this be women? A better plan would be
    For men to come to your temples and put down a price
    In bronze, or iron, or weight of gold, and buy their sons
    In embryo, for a sum befitting each man's wealth.
    Then they could live at home like free men – without women.
      Look – here's your proof that woman is an evil pest:
    Her father, who begot her and brought her up, then adds
    A dowry for her; this gets her a home, and he
    Gets rid of his load. The man who takes this noxious weed
    Into his home now rapturously decks his idol
    With gauds and gowns, heaps beauty on hatefulness, poor
      wretch,
    Squandering the family fortune. A woman should have
    No servant ever come near her; she should live attended
    By dumb and savage beasts; then she could neither speak
    To anyone, nor have any servant reply to her.
    As it is, unchaste wives brood on unchastity
    At home, while servants traffic their lewdness to the world –
    Yes, you, for one, who come here like a she-devil
    Inviting me to incest with my father's wife!
    I'll flush my ears with water to purge your filthy words!
    Do you think I could so sin, when even hearing you
    I feel polluted? One thing saves you, woman: I fear
    The gods. You trapped me, and I rashly gave my oath;
    Otherwise I'd have told my father the whole story.
    Instead, I shall now leave this house till he comes back;
    And I'll say nothing; but I shall come back with him,
    And observe how you – yes, and your mistress – meet his eye.

American/New York
young

Kennedy's Children

Robert Patrick

First presented at Clark Center for the Performing Arts-
Playwrights Horizons in New York City and at the King's Head,
Islington in 1974. The theme of the play is the death of the idea
of heroes as guides for our lives and the form is fragmentation
and separation of people from one another. It is set in a bar in
Lower East Side, New York City. MARK is an intense young
man, dressed in jeans and faded army jacket. He is sitting at a
table reading from a tattered notebook – the 'diary' he is writing
to his mother about his experience in Viet-Nam.

Published by Samuel French, London

Acts 1 and 2

MARK
Mom, I want to tell you about war, things nobody ever says about
it. I understand war, now. I have to do it in this diary, because
they read our mail, and besides, I think the beach may be bugged.
We have these men hiding in the jungle waiting to kill us. So have
they of course. They have us waiting to kill them. Because we have
invaded their country. But we are only trying to get earlier invaders
out of it. But they were only trying to get still earlier invaders out.
I don't know where it started. I don't know where it ends. I got
mad tonight and kicked over the little temple one of the fellas was
building out of seashells. I said, 'You killed a man today, Buster,
you ran him through with your bayonet and kicked him under the
philodendron like my mother has back home. You can't kill a man
in the morning and spend the night building little seashell temples
in the sand.' And I wanted to fight. But then I couldn't. Fighting
is so awful. Chick gave me a Librium and talked to me until I

72

calmed down. Chick is wonderful. He laughs when I say it but he is my spiritual advisor. I am becoming very spiritual, Mom. Chick is introducing me to oriental religion . . .

Mom, I want you to give this to the newspapers in case I am killed. This is what I really feel. The world must be one world, Mom. That is why *I* continue the war. If I did not, then the Viet Cong would overrun the world. And I am not sure of their aims. I am afraid of their leaders. I am afraid of our leaders too, but at least I know what their aims are. I think. Chick is helping me. He says we can't not fight because then we would be killed and die for others' causes. But we are killing men for the sake of ours. Chick says we must not think of it that way. He says we must only fight to save our lives, and not for any cause. He says it is beyond our control. But I am deceiving Chick. I am fighting to make the world one. I cannot sacrifice myself but I am sacrificing – no, I am not. I am getting confused. I have to fight for what I believe in. I must be very sure to understand what I believe in. It will not help to make the world one if it is an evil, misguided world. But isn't that what the other side wants? I don't know. Maybe it doesn't matter what people believe, as long as they all believe the same thing. I mustn't jump to conclusions. I must love everybody and I must kill the men that come at me every day and night out of the jungle. That's what the government says, that's what the Church says, that's what Chick says, and that's what I say. That is what Buddha says to me in my visions, too. I don't understand it. I'll do it. I've been doing it. I did it today. I'll keep on doing it. But I don't understand. Chick understands.

French
young

King John

William Shakespeare

The date of this historical play is uncertain. LEWIS, the Dauphin, is the historical Louis (VIII) and son of Philip II of France. To bring about peace with France a marriage is arranged between him and King John's niece, Blanche of Spain. However, the peace is short-lived. Pandulph, a papal legate, excommunicates John and urges Philip and the Dauphin to recommence war. To regain the support of Rome, John surrenders his crown to the papal legate and Pandulph orders LEWIS, who is by now encamped at St Edmundsbury, to stop fighting. LEWIS refuses to listen saying he has gone too far to turn back now.

Act 5, scene 2

LEWIS

Your Grace shall pardon me, I will not back:
I am too high-born to be propertied,
To be a secondary at control,
Or useful serving-man and instrument
To any sovereign state throughout the world.
Your breath first kindled the dead coal of wars
Between this chastis'd kingdom and myself
And brought in matter that should feed this fire;
And now 'tis far too huge to be blown out
With that same weak wind which enkindled it.
You taught me how to know the face of right,
Acquainted me with interest to this land,
Yea, thrust this enterprise into my heart;
And come ye now to tell me John hath made
His peace with Rome? What is that peace to me?
I, by the honour of my marriage-bed,
After young Arthur, claim this land for mine;
And, now it is half-conquer'd, must I back
Because that John hath made his peace with Rome?
Am I Rome's slave? What penny hath Rome borne,
What men provided, what munition sent,
To underprop this action? Is't not I
That undergo this charge? Who else but I,
And such as to my claim are liable,
Sweat in this business and maintain this war?
Have I not heard these islanders shout out
'Vive le roi!' as I have bank'd their towns?
Have I not here the best cards for the game
To win this easy match, play'd for a crown?
And shall I now give o'er the yielded set?
No, no, on my soul, it never shall be said.

American
23

Long Day's Journey into Night

Eugene O'Neill

Written in 1940 and produced at the Royal Dramatic Theatre, Stockholm in 1956 and later that year at the Helen Hayes Theater, New York. It is set in the summer of 1912 and is auto-biographical, recreating O'Neill's own painful family experiences. EDMUND, youngest son of the Tyrone family, has just been informed that he has consumption and that his father has arranged for him to go to Hilltown Sanitorium. In this scene, he and his father have been drinking all evening, trying to blot out the realisation that EDMUND's mother is becoming a hopeless morphine addict. EDMUND blames his father for her condition, accusing him of being too mean to pay for a proper cure. Moreover, he has found out that the Hilltown Sanitorium is a state institution – another example of his father's 'stinginess'. He is forever crying poverty, but can still afford another 'bum' property deal.

Published by Nick Hern Books, London

Act 4

EDMUND

And then you went to the Club to meet McGuire and let him stick you with another bum piece of property! (*As Tyrone starts to deny.*) Don't lie about it! We met McGuire in the hotel bar after he left you. Jamie kidded him about hooking you, and he winked and laughed!

[TYRONE (*lying feebly*). He's a liar if he said –]

EDMUND Don't lie about it! (*With gathering intensity.*) God, Papa, ever since I went to sea and was on my own, and found out what hard work for little pay was, and what it felt like to be broke, and starve, and camp on park benches because I had no place to sleep, I've tried to be fair to you because I knew what you'd been up against as a kid. I've tried to make allowances. Christ, you have to make allowances in this damned family or go nuts! I have tried to make allowances for myself when I remember all the rotten stuff I've pulled! I've tried to feel like Mama that you can't help being what you are where money is concerned. But God Almighty, this last stunt of yours is too much! It makes me want to puke! Not because of the rotten way you're treating me. To hell with that! I've treated you rottenly, in my way, more than once. But to think when it's a question of your son having consumption, you can show yourself up before the whole town as a stinking old tightwad! Don't you know Hardy will talk and the whole damned town will know? Jesus, Papa, haven't you any pride or shame? (*Bursting with rage.*) And I don't think I'll let you get away with it! I won't go to any damned state farm just to save you a few lousy dollars to buy more bum property with! You stinking old miser –! (*He chokes huskily, his voice trembling with rage, and then is shaken by a fit of coughing.*)

Set in Germany
middle-aged

Luther

John Osborne

First performed at the Theatre Royal, Nottingham in 1961 by
the English Stage Company. This scene is set in a market place
in 1517. A procession approaches, at its head the Pontiff's bull
of grace on cushion and cloth of gold, then the arms of the
Pope and the Medici, and after this JOHN TETZEL, Dominican,
inquisitor and most famed and successful indulgence vendor of
his day. A middle-aged professional huckster, able to winkle
coppers out of the pockets of the poor and desperate. He
addresses the crowd.

Published by Faber & Faber, London

Act 2, scene 1

TETZEL

Are you wondering who I am, or what I am? Is there anyone here among you, any small child, any cripple, or any sick idiot who hasn't heard of me, and doesn't know why I am here? No? No? Well, speak up then if there is? What, no one? Do you all know me then? Do you all know who I am? If it's true, it's very good, and just as it should be. Just as it should be, and no more than that! However, however – just in case – just in case, mind, there is one blind, maimed midget among you today who can't hear, I will open his ears and wash them out with sacred soap for him! And, as for the rest of you. I know I can rely on you all to listen patiently while I instruct him. Is that right? Can I go on? I'm asking you, is that right, can I go on? I say 'can I go on'?

(*Pause*)

Thank you. And what is there to tell this blind, maimed midget who's down there somewhere among you? No, don't look round for him, you'll only scare him and then he'll lose his one great chance, and it's not likely to come again, or if it does come, maybe it'll be too late. Well, what's the good news on this bright day? What's the information you want? It's this! Who is this friar with his red cross? Who sent him, and what's he here for? Don't try to work it out for yourself because I'm going to tell you now, this very minute. I am John Tetzel, Dominican, inquisitor, sub-commissioner to the Archbishop of Mainz, and what I bring you is indulgences. Indulgences made possible by the red blood of Jesus Christ, and the red cross you see standing up here behind me is the standard of those who carry them. Look at it! Go on, look at it! What else do you see hanging from the red cross? Well, what do they look like? Why, it's the arms of his holiness, because why? Because it's him who sent me here. Yes, my friend, the Pope himself has sent me with indulgences for you! Fine, you say, but what are indulgences? And what are they to me? What are indulgences? They're only the most precious and noble of God's gifts to men, that's all they are! Before God, I tell you I wouldn't swap my privilege at this moment with that of St. Peter in Heaven because I've already saved more souls with my indulgences than he could ever have done with all his sermons.

Swedish
40s

A Map of the World

David Hare

First performed at the Lyttleton Theatre, London in 1983. The
play opens in the lounge of a hotel in Bombay, where diplomats
and journalists are gathering for a UNESCO conference on World
Poverty. MARTINSON is a tall, grave and persistent Swede in
his forties. His apparent doggedness turns out to have an iron
quality. He is determined that the conference will be a success.
In this scene he is trying to persuade the guest speaker, Victor
Mehta, to read out a short statement on the nature of fiction
before giving his address, thereby pacifying some of the diplomats from those countries who have felt insulted by certain
remarks made in Victor's books.

Published in *The Asian Plays*, by Faber & Faber, London

Act 1

MARTINSON

We are here to discuss world poverty. The conference has taken many years to assemble, and in a week's time, the reluctant governments of the West will return home and try to forget they have ever attended. It is true. Any excuse they can find to dismiss the whole occasion as a shambles they will seize on and exploit. Therefore it is, without question, essential that the conference is given every chance of life, every chance of success. If Mr Mehta refuses to read out this little concoction, then he will make a fine gesture of individual conscience against the pressures – I will say this and please do not repeat it – of less than scrupulous groups, and he will go home to Shropshire, and he will feel proud and clever and generally excellent. And *Time* magazine will write of him, yes, and there will be editorials on the bloody writer's freedom, hurrah! But the conference will be destroyed. It is a short statement, it is an unimportant statement, because it is on a subject which is of no conceivable general interest or importance, namely, what a novel is, which I can hardly see is a subject of vital and continuing fascination to the poor. Frankly, who cares? is my attitude, and I think you will find it is the attitude of all the non-aligned countries . . . (*He looks behind him for confirmation, and the diplomats all nod.*) Certainly, the Scandinavian bloc . . .

[DIPLOMATS Yes . . . Indeed, it is our attitude.]

MARTINSON What is your phrase? We do not give a toss what a novel is. I think I may even say this is Scandinavia's official position, and if a man stands up at the beginning of this afternoon's session and lies about what a novel is, I will just be grateful because then there is a better chance that aid will flow, because grain will flow, because water will flow . . .

Senegalese
30s

A Map of the World

David Hare

First performed at the Lyttleton Theatre, London in 1983. The play opens in the lounge of a hotel in Bombay, where diplomats and journalists are gathering for a UNESCO conference on World Poverty. M'BENGUE is a Senegalese in his thirties, who has helped to draft a short statement on the nature of fiction, for the guest speaker, writer Victor Mehta, to read out before his main address. Mehta refuses to do this and M'BENGUE accuses him of distorting the facts in his novels in order to make fun of other less important governments and nations.

Published in *The Asian Plays*, by Faber & Faber, London

Act 1

M'BENGUE

We take aid from the West because we are poor, and in everything we are made to feel our inferiority. The price you ask us to pay is not money but misrepresentation. The way the nations of the West make us pay is by representing us continually in their organs of publicity as bunglers and murderers and fools. I have spent time in England and there the yellow press does not speak of Africa except to report how a nun has been raped, or there has been a tribal massacre, or how we are slaughtering the elephants – the elephants who are so much more suitable for television programmes than the Africans – or how corrupt and incompetent such-and-such a government is. If the crop succeeds, it is not news. If we build a dam, it is called boring. 'Oh, we do not report the building of dams,' say your newspapers. Dam-building is dull. Boring. The white man's word for everything with which he does not wish to come to terms. Yes, he will give us money, but the price we will pay is that he will not seek to understand our point of view. Pro-Moscow, pro-Washington, that is the only way you can see the world. All your terms are political, and your politics is the crude fight between your two great blocs. Is Angola pro-Russian? Is it pro-American? These are the only questions you ever ask yourselves. As if the whole world could be seen in those terms. In your terms. In the white man's terms and through the white man's media.

Indian
40s

A Map of the World

David Hare

First performed at the Lyttleton Theatre, London in 1983. It is
set in the lounge of a hotel in Bombay, where a UNESCO conference on World Poverty is about to take place. VICTOR MEHTA,
an important, but controversial Indian writer, invited as guest
speaker, and Stephen Andrews, a young journalist from a left
wing magazine, are openly hostile to one another from the out-
set. Both are attracted to Peggy, a young American actress staying at the hotel. A contest is set up whereby the two men argue
their viewpoints. Elaine, a journalist from CBS, agrees to adjudi-
cate. The winner will sleep with Peggy. Stephen opens the
argument and MEHTA is reluctantly drawn in.

Published in *The Asian Plays*, Faber & Faber, London

Act 2

MEHTA

It seems when people become prosperous, they lose the urge to improve themselves. Anyone who comes new to a society, as I did, an immigrant, has his priorities clear: to succeed in that society, to seek practical achievement, to educate his children to the highest level. Yet somehow once one or two generations have established their success, their grandchildren rush the other way, to disown that success, to disown its responsibilities, to seek by dressing as savages and eating brown rice to discredit the very civilization their grandfathers worked so hard to create. This seems to me the ultimate cruelty . . .

[PEGGY Yes . . .]

MEHTA . . . the ultimate charade: that the young in the West should dare to turn their faces at this time to the Third World and cast doubt on the value of their own material prosperity. Not content with flaunting its wealth, the West now fashionably pretends that the materialism that has produced this wealth is not a good thing. Well, at least give us a chance to find out, say the poor. For God's sake let us practise this contempt ourselves. Instead of sending the Third World doctors and mechanics, we now send them hippies, and Marxist thinkers, and animal conservationists, and ecologists, and wandering fake Zen Buddhist students, who hasten to reassure the illiterate that theirs is a superior life to that of the West. What hypocrisy! The marriage of the decadent with the primitive, the faithless with the barbarian. Reason overthrown, as it is now overthrown all over the world! An unholy alliance, approved, sanctified and financed by this now futile United Nations.

[STEPHEN Futile? Why futile?]

MEHTA Futile because it no longer does any good.

Black South African
40s

Master Harold and the Boys

Athol Fugard

Performed at the Market Theatre, Johannesburg in 1983 and later that year at the National Theatre in London. The scene opens in the St George's Park tea room on a wet and windy Port Elizabeth afternoon in 1950. WILLIE, a black man in his forties, is on his hands and knees mopping the floor. He has his sleeves and trousers rolled up. He sings as he works and talks to Sam, a waiter who is looking through a pile of comics.

Published in *Athol Fugard Selected Plays*, by Oxford University Press, Oxford

Act 1

WILLIE
(*Singing as he works*).

> 'She was scandalizin' my name,
> She took my money
> She called me honey
> But she was scandalizin' my name.
> Called it love but was playin' a game . . .'

(*He gets up and moves the bucket. Stands thinking for a moment, then, raising his arms to hold an imaginary partner, he launches into an intricate ballroom dance step. Although a mildly comic figure, he reveals a reasonable degree of accomplishment.*)
Hey, Sam.
(*Sam, absorbed in the comic book, does not respond.*)
Hey, *Boet* Sam!
(*Sam looks up.*)
I'm getting it. The quickstep. Look now and tell me. (*He repeats the step.*) Well? . . .
How can I enjoy myself? Not straight, too stiff and now it's also

86

glide, give it more style, make it smooth . . . *Haai!* Is hard to remember all those things, *Boet* Sam . . . I got no romance left for Hilda anymore . . . I know, I know! (*To the jukebox.*) I do it better with music. You got sixpence for Sarah Vaughan? . . . I only got bus fare to go home. (*He returns disconsolately to his work.*) Love story and happy ending! She's doing it all right, *Boet* Sam, but is not me she's giving happy endings. Fuckin' whore! Three nights now she doesn't come practise. I wind up gramophone, I get record ready and I sit and wait. What happens? Nothing. Ten o'clock I start dancing with my pillow. You try and practise romance by yourself, *Boet* Sam. 'Struesgod, she doesn't come tonight I take back my dress and ballroom shoes and I find me new partner. Size twenty-six. Shoes size seven. And now she's also making trouble for me with the baby again. Reports me to Child Wellfed, that I'm not giving her money. She lies! Every week I am giving her money for milk. And how do I know is my baby? Only his hair looks like me. She's fucking around all the time I turn my back. Hilda Samuels is a bitch! (*Pause.*) Hey, Sam! . . . You listening? . . . She is not too bad with the waltz, *Boet* Sam. Is the quickstep where the trouble starts . . . Legs. That's her trouble. She can't move them quick enough, *Boet* Sam. I start the record and before halfway Count Basie is already winning. Only time we catch up with him is when gramophone runs down.
(*Sam laughs.*)
Haaikona, Boet Sam, is not funny.

Haai	no! or well I never!
Boet	brother or pal
Haaikona	emphatic 'no' or 'oh no'

Black South African
40s

Master Harold and the Boys

Athol Fugard

Performed at the Market Theatre, Johannesburg in 1983 and later that year at the National Theatre in London. The scene opens in the St George's Park tea room on a wet and windy Port Elizabeth afternoon in 1950. SAM, a black waiter in his forties, has been closer to Hally, a young white boy and son of the tea room proprietress, than Hally's own parents. Now they quarrel and Hally spits in SAM's face. SAM reminds Hally of their early days together when he made him a kite so that he had something to look up to.

Published in *Selected Plays*, by Oxford University Press, Oxford

Act 1

SAM (*to Hally*).
You don't know all of what you've just done . . . Master Harold
. . . A long time ago I promised myself I was going to try and do
something, but you've just shown me . . . Master Harold . . . that
I've failed. (*Pause.*) I've also got a memory of a little white boy when
he was still wearing short trousers, and a black man, but they're
not flying a kite. It was the old Jubilee days, after dinner one night.
I was in my room. You came in and just stood against the wall,
looking down at the ground, and only after I'd asked you what
you wanted, what was wrong, I don't know how many times, did
you speak and even then so softly I almost didn't hear you. 'Sam,
please help me to go and fetch my Dad.' Remember? He was dead
drunk on the floor of the Central Hotel Bar. They'd phoned for
your Mom, but you were the only one at home. And do you remember how we did it? You went in first by yourself to ask permission
for me to go into the bar. Then I loaded him on to my back like a
baby and carried him back to the boarding house with you following
behind carrying his crutches. (*Shaking his head as he remembers.*) A
crowded Main Street with all the people watching a little white boy
following his drunk father on a kaffir's back! I felt for that little boy
. . . Master Harold. I felt for him . . . It would have been so simple
if you could have just despised him for being a weak man. But
he's your father. You love him and you're ashamed of him. You're
ashamed of so much! . . . And now that's going to include yourself.
That was the promise I made to myself: to try and stop that happen-
ing. (*Pause.*) . . . If you really want to know, that's why I made you
that kite. I wanted you to look up, be proud of something, of
yourself . . . (*Bitter smile at the memory.*) . . . and you certainly were
that when I left you with it up there on the hill. Oh, *ja* . . . something else! . . . If you ever do write it as a short story, there *was* a
twist in our ending. I couldn't sit down there and stay with you.
It was a 'Whites Only' bench. You were too young, too excited to
notice then. But not anymore. If you're not careful . . . Master
Harold . . . you're going to be sitting up there by yourself for a
long time to come, and there won't be a kite in the sky. (*Sam has
got nothing more to say. He exits into the kitchen, taking off his waiter's
jacket.*)

Moroccan
young/middle-aged

The Merchant of Venice

William Shakespeare

Possibly written in about 1596, the action of this comedy moves
between the harsh business world of Antonio's Venice and the
gracious world of Portia's Belmont, where suitors from far and
wide come to woo this rich and beautiful heiress. The first of
these is the PRINCE OF MOROCCO, who arrives with his train,
and having declared his love for Portia, prepares to try his hand
in the lottery devised by her father of three caskets of gold,
silver and lead, whereby whoever chooses the right casket wins
her hand in marriage.

Act 2, scene 1

PRINCE OF MOROCCO

    Mislike me not for my complexion,
    The shadowed livery of the burnish'd sun,
    To whom I am a neighbour, and near bred.
    Bring me the fairest creature northward born,
    Where Phœbus' fire scarce thaws the icicles,
    And let us make incision for your love
    To prove whose blood is reddest, his or mine.
    I tell thee, lady, this aspect of mine
    Hath fear'd the valiant; by my love, I swear
    The best-regarded virgins of our clime
    Have lov'd it too. I would not change this hue,
    Except to steal your thoughts, my gentle queen . . .
    Even for that I thank you.
    Therefore, I pray you, lead me to the caskets
    To try my fortune. By this scimitar,
    That slew the Sophy and a Persian prince,
    That won three fields of Sultan Solyman,
    I would o'erstare the sternest eyes that look,
    Outbrave the heart most daring on the earth,
    Pluck the young sucking cubs from the she-bear,
    Yea, mock the lion when 'a roars for prey,
    To win thee, lady. But, alas the while!
    If Hercules and Lichas play at dice
    Which is the better man, the greater throw
    May turn by fortune from the weaker hand.
    So is Alcides beaten by his page;
    And so may I, blind Fortune leading me,
    Miss that which one unworthier may attain,
    And die with grieving.

Australian
40s

Night and Day

Tom Stoppard

First presented at the Phoenix Theatre, London in 1978 and set
in a fictitious African country, where war is likely to break out
at any moment. In this scene, WAGNER, an Australian journalist
in his forties, working for the *Sunday Globe*, complains to his
photographer, Guthrie, that he has been scooped by his own
paper.

Published by Faber & Faber, London

Act 1

WAGNER
Didn't you know about my famous scoop?

[GUTHRIE No.]

WAGNER Nor did I. Sunday, everyone gets cables. 'Globe finds
Colonel Shimbu. Why Colonel unfound by you', etcetera. So everybody's screaming, where is he, Wagner, you bastard? Only, it isn't
my story. *I* don't know where the bloody Colonel is. So they want
to see my cable – they think it's a herogram from Hammaker. But
of course I can't show it to them because I don't know what this
happy birthday thing is all about. So then they're calling me a
lying bastard, and following me to the lavatory when they aren't
following armoured car patrols into the bush in broken-down taxis.
You never saw anything like it.

[GUTHRIE Yes I did.]

WAGNER Yes you did. There's a government press officer here who's
the usual lying jerk, but there's no way of telling whether he's lying
because he knows the truth or because he doesn't know anything,

so you can't trust his mendacity either – he could be telling the truth half the time, by accident. His line was that the Adoma Liberation Front didn't exist, and the army had got it completely surrounded. But the *Sunday Globe* knocked that one on the head. We heard it on the radio, the BBC World Service picked it up. And what do you know, George? – some sodding little stringer with no name has found Colonel Shimbu and made a monkey out of me. Yeah. It sounded like a good piece, too. I'd like to know how he got the story out. Interview with the Colonel himself, a party political broadcast wouldn't have done it better, and furthermore it's not a rebellion, it's a secession – get the picture? *Media credibility!* Well, the press officer goes bananas. He wants to know which side the *Globe* thinks it's on. So I tell him, it's not on any side, stupid, it's an objective fact-gathering organization. And he says, yes, but is it objective-for or objective-against? (*Pause*) He may be stupid, but he's not stupid.

[GUTHRIE I've got a present for you.]

(*Guthrie gets up and walks towards the back of the room where he picks up a pile of newspapers. Wagner doesn't turn to see this.*)

WAGNER So he spends the briefing attacking the *Globe* – God bless him, it's the only story I've filed this week – and he's in a flat spin trying to make everything fit. At the end, this very smooth guy from Reuters says, 'Let me see if I've got this right. It's not a *political* movement, it's just a lot – or rather *not* a lot – of completely illiterate ivory poachers who've been reading too much Marxist propaganda, and they're all armed with home-made weapons flown by Cuban pilots.'

[GUTHRIE (*Coming back*) Who's the *Globe* special correspondent?]

WAGNER I don't know. I'm famous in Jeddu. Scooped by my own paper.

African
50

Night and Day

Tom Stoppard

First presented at the Phoenix Theatre, London in 1978 and set in a fictitious African country where war is likely to break out at any moment. PRESIDENT MAGEEBA of Kambawe, a British-educated, unpredictable black African, has arranged to use the Carsons' residence as a halfway house for his proposed meeting with his rival, Colonel Shimbu. He has just arrived and is talking informally to his hosts and the journalist, Wagner, who has gate-crashed the meeting, hoping to obtain an interview for his paper. The Carsons ask Wagner to leave, but MAGEEBA insists that he stays.

Published by Faber & Faber, London

Act 2

MAGEEBA
At the time of independence the *Daily Citizen* was undoubtedly free. It was free to select the news it thought fit to print, to make much of it, or little, and free to make room for more and more girls wearing less and less underwear. You may smile, but does freedom of the press mean freedom to choose its own standards?

[CARSON Absolutely.]

MAGEEBA Mrs Carson?

[RUTH What's the alternative?]

MAGEEBA That was the question. Easy enough to shut the paper down, as I would have been obliged to do had it not been *burned* down during the state of emergency which followed independence. But what to put in its place? The English millionaire folded his

94

singed tents and stole away the insurance money, which didn't belong to him since I had nationalized the paper well before the fire was out. Never mind – the field was open. I did not believe a newspaper should be part of the apparatus of the state; we are not a totalitarian society. But neither could I afford a return to the whims of private enterprise. I had the immense and delicate task of restoring confidence in Kambawe. I could afford the naked women but not the naked scepticism, the carping and sniping and the public washing of dirty linen which represents freedom to an English editor. What then? A democratic committee of journalists? – a thorn bush for the editor to hide in. No, no – freedom with responsibility, that was the elusive formula we pondered all those years ago at the LSE. And that is what I found. From the ashes there arose, by public subscription, a new *Daily Citizen*, responsible and relatively free. (*He leans towards Wagner.*) Do you know what I mean by a relatively free press, Mr Wagner?

[WAGNER Not exactly, sir, no.]

MAGEEBA I mean a free press which is edited by one of my relatives. (*He throws back his head and laughs. Wagner joins in uncertainly. Ruth smiles nervously. Carson looks scared. Mageeba brings the weighted end of his stick down on Wagner's head.*)
(*Shouting*) So it doesn't go crawling to uppity niggers! – so it doesn't let traitors shit on the front page! – so it doesn't go sucking up to liars and criminals! 'Yes sir, Colonel Shimbu, tell us about the exploitation of your people! – free speech for all here, Colonel Shimbu, tell us about the wonderful world you're going to build in that vulture's garbage dump you want to call a country' – yes, you tell us before you get a machine-gun up your backside and your brains coming down your nostrils! – who's going to interview you *then*, Colonel, sir!
(*Mageeba has stood up and moved away from Wagner. Wagner's head is bleeding slightly above the hairline.*)
(*Evenly*) I'll give him equal space. Six foot long and six foot deep, just like any other traitor and communist jackal.

Welsh
young

Night Must Fall

Emlyn Williams

First produced at the Duchess Theatre, London in 1935. DANNY, a young Welshman with a rough accent, known as 'Baby-face', works at the Tallboys Hotel. He charms his way into old Mrs Bramson's household, and although her niece, Olivia, suspects that he has already murdered a woman staying at the Tallboys, he manages to keep her quiet until he kills again – this time old Mrs Bramson herself. In this scene he is talking to Olivia about his victims and boasting that he will never be caught. She is fascinated by him, in spite of herself, and he knows it.

Published by Heinemann, Oxford

Act 3, scene 2

DAN (*realises his hands are wet with paraffin and wipes them on his trousers.*)
Clumsy . . .

[OLIVIA I never expected to come across it in real life.]

DAN (*lightly*) You didn't ought to read so much. I never got through a book yet . . . But I'll read you all right . . . (*Crossing to her, leaning over the table, and smiling at her intently.*) You haven't had a drop of drink, and yet you feel as if you had. You never knew there was such a secret part inside of you. All that book-learnin' and moral-me-eye here and social-me-eye there – you took that off on the edge of the wood same as if it was an overcoat . . . and you left it there!

[OLIVIA I hate you. I . . . hate you!]

DAN (*urgently*) And same as anybody out for the first time without their overcoat, you feel as light as air! Same as I feel, sometimes – only I never had no overcoat —— (*Excited.*) Why – this is my big chance! You're the one I can tell about meself! Oh, I'm sick o' hearin' how clever everybody else is – I want to tell 'em how clever *I* am for a change! . . . Money I'm going to have, and people doin' what they're told, and *me* tellin' them to do it! There was a 'oman at the Tallboys, wasn't there? She wouldn't be told, would she? She thought she was up 'gainst a soft fellow in a uniform, didn't she? She never knew it was *me* she was dealin' with – (*striking his chest in a paroxysm of elation*) – Me! And this old girl treatin' me like a son 'cause I made her think she was a chronic invalid – ha! She's been more use to me tonight (*tapping the notes in his jacket pocket, smartly*) than she has to any other body all her life. Stupid, that's what people are . . . stupid. If those two hadn't been stupid they might be breathin' now; you're not stupid; that's why I'm talkin' to you. (*With exaggerated self-possession.*) You said just now murder's ordinary . . . Well it isn't ordinary at all, see? And I'm not an ordinary chap. There's one big difference 'tween me and other fellows that try this game. I'll *never be found out*. 'Cause I don't care a —— (*snapping his fingers, grandly.*) The world's goin' to hear from me. That's me. (*Chuckling.*) You wait . . . (*After a pause.*) But you can't wait, can you?

Welsh
18

Nil Carborundum

Henry Livings

First presented by the Royal Shakespeare Company in 1962 at
the Arts Theatre, London. It is set on an RAF Station where a
mock invasion exercise is about to take place. TAFFY JONES
works in the kitchen, a monumental mason by trade, he is use-
less as a waiter. He is willing and kind, even to those who
torment him. As Operation 'Shatter' begins, he enters carrying
two rifles, one of which he hands to Neville, the new cook. He
chatters on to Neville and Albert, the other cook, against the
clicking of rifles and occasional thunderflash.

Published by Penguin Books, London

Act 3

TAFFY
Hey Nev! Nev!

> [NEVILLE (*enters, watching the troops with considerable interest*) What's
> up with everyone?]

TAFFY Here I brought you your rifle from the billet.

> [NEVILLE Why?]

TAFFY Didn't you know there's a war on? Mr McKendrick says will
you be ready with egg and chips for the sergeants during the night.
And tea. And pay special attention to the needs of the mess waiter
he says.

> [NEVILLE Soldiers?]

TAFFY That's right, Nev boyo. Here you are (*the rifle*). That there
little hole at the end is where the bullets come out as I remember.
I've an idea the C.O. knows there's a war on too . . . we nearly

had our first casualty just now, missed me by inches as I was coming up the road. Brings out the whole drama of battle when you drive fast don't it? Only I don't think I'm a hero, because I skipped out of the way pretty quick.

(*Albert comes mooching by on his way to the Mess.*)

'Do unto others as you would be done by yourself', tha's what they say don't they? Well how'd you cope with a fellow like our C.O. who ain't bothered whether it's him or another who gets battered into little pieces? I think he's an anti-social element and irreligious into the bargain. Perhaps I ought to shoot him with one o'my imaginary bullets and let him imagine he's dead. Oh hello Bert you better get yourself a gun or you won't make a realistic target for the enemy.

(*Albert lours. He and Neville move into the kitchen to escape Taffy's barrage of chatter.*)

Well I'll be seeing you lads. Me and the others have got to fall into line and be shot at.

(*Taffy pauses briefly and we hear the clicking of rifle bolts that fills the air like crickets.*)

Just listen to them rifles clicking. Sinister innit? But don't worry chaps, they're ours.

(*A thunderflash goes off close by.*)

That's them bloody rotten umpires. I seen 'em sneaking about with them fireworks. I prefer the enemy. I mean you can't even surrender to an umpire can you? Bye now. (*Taffy goes.*)

Irish
middle-aged

Once a Catholic

Mary O'Malley

First performed at the Royal Court Theatre, London in 1977 and
set in the Convent of Our Lady of Fatima – a Grammar School for
Girls, and in and around the streets of Willesden and Harlesden,
London NW10, from September, 1956 to July, 1957. FATHER
MULLARKEY is a Catholic priest who has come to hear Form
Five A's catechism and talk to them about the importance of
Purity.

Published by Amber Lane Press, Oxford

Act 1, scene 9

FATHER MULLARKEY

Good. Now I want to say a little word to you about the vital importance of purity. You're all getting to be big girls now. Indeed some of you are bigger than others. Isn't it a great joy to be young and healthy with all your life before you. Sooner or later you might want to share your life with a member of the opposite sex. The best way to find a boyfriend is to join a Catholic Society where you'll have scope for all sorts of social activities. Now when you've met your good Catholic boy and you're getting to know each other he might suggest a bit of a kiss and a cuddle. Well, let him wait. And if he doesn't want to wait let him go. Any cuddling and kissing is bound to arouse bad feelings and desires for the intimate union allowed only in Matrimony. (*He bangs on the desk.*) The intimate union of the sexes is a sacred act. A duty to be done in a state of grace by a man and his wife and nobody else. So until the day you kneel at the altar with a bridal veil on your head you must never be left alone in a room with a boyfriend. Or in a field for that matter. Let the two of you go out and about with other young couples to dances and to parties and the like. But a particular word of warning about the latter. There's no doubt at all that alcoholic drinks make a party go with a swing. The danger is that after a couple of drinks a boy and a girl are more inclined to take liberties with each other. To indulge in such liberties is sinful. The girl has the special responsibility in the matter because a boy's passions are more readily aroused, God help him. Show your affection by all means. But keep to holding hands with an occasional kiss on the cheek. A Catholic boy, in his heart of hearts, will be impressed by such insistence on perfect chastity. Ask Our Blessed Lady to keep you free from the temptations of the flesh. And make no mistake about it, a passionate kiss on the lips between a boy and a girl is a serious mortal sin. (*He bangs on the desk.*) When you've the wedding ring on your finger you can fire away to your heart's content. Now has any girl any question she'd like to ask?

London
late teens

Once a Catholic

Mary O'Malley

First performed at the Royal Court Theatre, London in 1977 and set in the Convent of Our Lady of Fatima – a Grammar School for Girls, and in and around the streets of Willesden and Harlesden, London, NW10, from September, 1956 to July, 1957.

DEREK is a tall, thin Teddy boy in his late teens, with ambitions of becoming a train driver. He has been going out with Mary McGinty, a fifth former from the Convent, for two and a half weeks. In this scene they are standing on the street corner. He has just tried to kiss her, but she turns her head away. 'A passionate kiss on the lips is a serious mortal sin.' DEREK is 'C of E' and mortal sins mean nothing to him. He reckons Mary takes her religion a bit too seriously.

Published by Amber Lane Press, Oxford

Act 1, scene 12

DEREK

Yeah, well, that's what I stick down if I have to fill up a form for something or other. C of E. It don't mean nothing, do it, except you're an ordinary English person. It's hard luck for you, ain't it, having an Irish Mum and Dad. You know, you don't strike me as being one bit Irish yourself. I mean, you could easy pass yourself off as a normal person. Funny how you can spot a mick a mile off. No offence to your old man or nothing. I mean, I've got nothing against them 'part from the fact that they drink too much and they're always picking fights among themselves. It makes me die laughing the way their hair stands all up on end. Half of them have got that diabolical ginger hair, ain't they. And all of them have got them big red faces. And them bleedin' great flapping trousers you see them wearing down the Kilburn High Road. You could fit half a dozen navvies into one leg alone. I never can understand a word they're saying. Bejasus and all that boloney. Myself I reckon they all take religion a bit too serious. I mean, you can understand it more with the Italians, having the Pope stuck in the Vatican there, keeping his eye on them. But the Irish are bleedin' miles away. Why should they have to take orders from the Pope? If I was you I'd be a bit suspicious of that Heaven you're so keen to get up to. It's gonna be packed out with some of the worst types of foreigners. The Irish'll be the only ones up there speaking English.

American/Southern
30

Orpheus Descending

Tennessee Williams

First presented at the Martin Beck Theater, New York in 1957
and set in a dry goods store in a small southern town. It is a
reworking of the Orpheus and Eurydice story, period 1940. VAL,
a young guitar player of about thirty, has just come into town
looking for work. In this scene he meets 'Lady', who is manag-
ing the store, while her elderly husband lies upstairs dying of
cancer.

Published by Penguin Books, London

Act 1

VAL
You might think there's many and many kinds of people in this world but, Lady, there's just two kinds of people, the ones that are bought and the buyers! No! – there's one other kind . . .

[LADY What kind's that?]

VAL The kind that's never been branded . . . You know they's a kind of bird that don't have legs so it can't light on nothing but has to stay all its life on its wings in the sky? That's true. I seen one once, it had died and fallen to earth and it was light-blue coloured and its body was tiny as your little finger, that's the truth, it had a body as tiny as your little finger and so light on the palm of your hand it didn't weigh more than a feather, but its wings spread out this wide but they were transparent, the colour of the sky and you could see through them. That's what they call protection colouring. Camouflage, they call it. You can't tell those birds from the sky and that's why the hawks don't catch them, don't see them up there in the high blue sky near the sun!

[LADY How about in grey weather?]

VAL They fly so high in grey weather the goddam hawks would get dizzy. But those little birds, they don't have no legs at all and they live their whole lives on the wing, and they sleep on the wind, that's how they sleep at night, they just spread their wings and go to sleep on the wind like other birds fold their wings and go to sleep on a tree . . . (*Music fades in.*) – They sleep on the wind and . . . (*His eyes grow soft and vague and he lifts his guitar and accompanies the very faint music.*) – never light on this earth but one time when they die.

[LADY I'd like to be one of those birds.]

VAL So'd I like to be one of those birds; they's lots of people would like to be one of those birds and never be – corrupted!

105

Irish/Donegal
young

Philadelphia, Here I Come!

Brian Friel

First performed at the Gaiety Theatre, Dublin in 1964 and set in the small village of Ballybeg in County Donegal, Ireland. The action takes place on the night before and on the morning of Gareth O'Donnell's departure for Philadelphia. There are two 'Gars' – the Public Gar is the one everyone sees, the PRIVATE Gar is the unseen man, the man within. In this scene PRIVATE remembers the day, fifteen years ago, when his father, known as 'Old Screwballs', took him fishing.

Published by Faber & Faber, London

Part 1, episode 3

(*Private and Public jump erect again and in perfect unison give out their decade. Gradually, as the prayers continue, they relax into their slumped position.*)

PRIVATE

When you're curled up in your wee cot, Screwballs, do you dream? Do you ever dream of the past, Screwballs, of that wintry morning in Bailtefree, and the three days in Bundoran? . . . (*Public stays as he is. Private gets slowly to his feet and moves over to S.B. He stands looking down at him.*)

. . . and of the young, gay girl from beyond the mountains who sometimes cried herself to sleep? (*Softly, nervously, with growing excitement.*) God – maybe – Screwballs – behind those dead eyes and that flat face are there memories of precious moments in the past? My God, have I been unfair to you? Is it possible that you have hoarded in the back of that mind of yours – do you remember – it was an afternoon in May – oh, fifteen years ago – I don't remember every detail but some things are as vivid as can be: the boat was blue and the paint was peeling and there was an empty cigarette packet floating in the water at the bottom between two trout and the left rowlock kept slipping and you had given me your hat and had put your jacket round my shoulders because there had been a shower of rain. And you had the rod in your left hand – I can see the cork nibbled away from the butt of the rod – and maybe we had been chatting – I don't remember – it doesn't matter – but between us at that moment there was this great happiness, this great joy – you must have felt it too – it was so much richer than a content – it was a great, great happiness, and active, bubbling joy – although nothing was being said – just the two of us fishing on a lake on a showery day – and young as I was I felt, I knew, that this was precious, and your hat was soft on the top of my ears – I can feel it – and I shrank down into your coat – and then, then for no reason at all except that you were happy too, you began to sing: (*sings*)

> All round my hat I'll wear a green coloured ribbono,
> All round my hat for a twelve month and a day.
> And if anybody asks me the reason why I wear it,
> It's all because my true love is far, far away.

Irish/West
young

The Playboy of the Western World

J.M. Synge

First performed at the Abbey Theatre, Dublin in 1907 and set in
the West of Ireland. CHRISTY MAHON, a young farm hand, has
quarrelled with his father, striking the old man down and leaving him for dead. Terrified, he has run away and taken refuge
in a country pub, or 'shebeen', run by Michael James and his
daughter Pegeen. As CHRISTY haltingly begins his tale and
Pegeen and the girls serve him with food and drink, it slowly
dawns on him that a 'young man who has killed his father' is
something of a curiosity among the 'locals' – even a hero to the
village girls – and in particular, Pegeen and the Widow Quinn.

Published by A & C Black, London

Act 2

CHRISTY

It's a long story; you'd be destroyed listening . . .

We were digging spuds in his cold, sloping, stony, divil's patch of a field . . .

There I was, digging and digging, and 'You squinting idiot,' says he, 'let you walk down now and tell the priest you'll wed the Widow Casey in a score of days' . . .

(*with horror*)

A walking terror from beyond the hills, and she two score and five years, and two hundredweights and five pounds in the weighing scales, with a limping leg on her, and a blinded eye, and she a woman of noted misbehaviour with the old and young . . .

(*eating with growing satisfaction*)

He was letting on I was wanting a protector from the harshness of the world, and he without a thought the whole while but how he'd have her hut to live in and her gold to drink . . .

'I won't wed her,' says I, 'when all know she did suckle me for six weeks when I came into the world, and she a hag this day with a tongue on her has the crows and seabirds scattered, the way they wouldn't cast a shadow on her garden with the dread of her curse' . . .

'She's too good for the like of you,' says he, 'and go on now or I'll flatten you out like a crawling beast has passed under a dray.' 'You will not if I can help it,' says I. 'Go on,' says he, 'or I'll have the divil making garters of your limbs tonight.' 'You will not if I can help it,' says I . . .

(*He sits up, brandishing his mug*)

(*impressively*)

With that the sun came out between the cloud and the hill, and it shining green in my face. 'God have mercy on your soul,' says he, lifting a scythe; 'or on your own,' says I, raising the loy . . .

(*flattered and confident, waving bone*)

He gave a drive with the scythe, and I gave a lep to the east. Then I turned around with my back to the north, and I hit a blow on the ridge of his skull, laid him stretched out, and he split to the knob of his gullet.

(*He raises the chicken bone to his Adam's apple*)

109

American/Irish
40s

A Prayer For My Daughter

Thomas Babe

Presented at the Public Theater, New York in 1978, it is set in the squad room of a downtown precinct. An old woman has been killed for 26 dollars. It is 1.00am and the suspects, Jimmy, almost a boy, and SEAN, in his forties, lean and bearded with something of the professor about him, are being grilled by two hard bitten cops, determined to extract a confession from one of them. SEAN is about to crack. He badly needs a fix and begins talking about what happened to him in Viet-Nam (and how he gave himself his first shot of morphine).

Published by Samuel French, London

Act 2

SEAN

A while ago, in Vietnam, in actual fact, I saw something, a man, and he was a soldier, well, everybody was a soldier but me, and I ignored them, I figured it was better not to know a single one of them personally because I might have to save his life and the pressure would've been wrong on me to save the life of a man I knew or maybe loved so I didn't. But there was this one man I didn't know, had never even ever seen before, sitting under a tree; he had his shirt off, he was all bloody and dirty from a fire fight, and he was doing nothing, just smoking a joint, and I was watching him the way I sometimes watched the men, thinking the dumbest crap, like how much I wanted to touch his shoulder, and he was nobody special at all and suddenly he turned toward me and waved and I thought, he must be waving at somebody behind me, so I turned around and saw there was nobody else but the two of us, and he waved again, and I started to be sort of pleased because I

110

could see his eyes were intelligent and kind, and then he pointed right at me, and I thought, what is this, does he like me, this stranger, and then he said something that I couldn't hear, and I think I smiled and made the I can't hear you gesture, so he stood up and started to shout and I still couldn't hear, but I wanted to, so then he stood all the way up and that's when I heard the shot and he was nailed in the neck by a sniper and dropped like a ton of bricks, and of course, the shooting started again and me, by instinct, crawled on my belly to him, to where I stuck a wad in his neck and turned him over and cradled his head in my lap and wiped the shit off his forehead, because I always comforted the men I knew I couldn't help who were going to die and then I realized, Christ on the bloody cross, you shit-bucket, you know you're going to weep, and so it was, for the first time ever, I opened my kit and gave myself a shot of morphine, and I sat there I'm told, for twelve hours, with his head in my lap, and he seemed to me to be an angel and every time I came out of it I fixed again. The sergeant said to me afterwards: shit, son, you were holdin onto that stiff so dear, goddamn if we didn't think we were gonna have to stuff the *both* of you in the body bag. (*Pause.*) Give me a hit, officer. Just a little hit, please . . . There's a woman inside me, officer, and she aches for the men she has known. She flirts with them and cries for them when they have to go in the morning; she likes to please them but she likes to have her cigarette lit, at least when I used to smoke . . . and I hate her so much that most often I want to kill her, because she loves her men so completely that it terrifies me . . . and she says to me, whenever I think there is no woman in me, that I am a liar and a fool, and she is the one who makes me cry and she's the one who makes me sing goddamn songs to men . . . live men, dead men, it doesn't matter. (*Pause.*) And he was her first, my woman, her first man. Nothing came of it but that I ran my fingers through his hair for, they tell me, twelve hours, and I sang:
YOU ARE MY SO FORTH
MY ONLY SO FORTH
YOU MAKE ME SO FORTH
(*Pause, Sean's tone changes slightly back to its old crispness.*) Does a word of this makes the least little sense to you?

Russian
late 50s

Retreat From Moscow

Don Taylor

Produced at the New End Theatre, London in 1993 – directed
by the author and set in present time. Tom, a lecturer in classics,
now redundant from his university, is delighted when his old
friend, BORIS ANDREYEVICH, a big bluff Russian bear of a man,
arrives unexpectedly on his doorstep with a suitcase full of secret
KGB documents, which he intends to publish and make them
both a lot of money. But things are not as they seem. Tom's
daughter finds packages of heroin in the suitcase, and BORIS
confesses that he has been a KGB informer for forty years and
has escaped from Moscow with the help of a KGB Colonel – the
price of his freedom being the heroin he has been forced to
smuggle into England.

Available on application to Samuel French, London

Act 2

BORIS

The gaps between the phone calls got longer, like remission from
a fatal disease. When Mikhail Sergeyevich came to power, they
stopped. Like everyone else, I celebrated. I thought the darkness
was over at last, and I too, like my country, could become free. But
no one is ever free . . . That afternoon at the Dacha you liked so
much, you found so Russian . . . I suspect that at least two of the
people you met there, the poet and the literary critic, were like me,
informers. You can never know of course. We don't all belong to
a club and wear a badge. But we smile at each other, and we know.
Why else do we enjoy such mild privileges? And you, my old
friend, thought we were a cell of dissidents . . . ! . . . The only way
out is to die, like my philosopher friend who drank himself to

112

death in a weekend. He knew they would never let him go, and he couldn't bear it any longer . . . No one is ever free from the past. They moved me around the country, second rate university to second rate university. I had just been appointed to Moscow at last, about the time we met. There, I was always terrified that I would meet people I had betrayed on the street, as they gradually came back from the camps. The ones who had survived . . . But nothing happened, till the August coup. It was wonderful, of course, but then, the KGB collapsed, and its files were being opened up. I was in those files, for forty years. I was terrified I would be denounced . . . I was beyond decisions by then. I am nearly sixty, and the life I have lived has blasted my moral fibre to pieces! It is like old frayed string, and will bear no kind of weight at all. But I got another phone call . . . This was quite a different proposition. He was a full KGB Colonel by then, but he hadn't forgotten my name, or my phone number. He told me he was getting out, and advised me to get out too, because very soon, all our actions would be public knowledge . . . He said he would get me out, and told me of his plan to make money in the West. He had access, for a few more days, to certain highly secret archives, we could get in together at night. But it would have to be soon. He was right about that. The day after we got them they were sealed and under guard . . . There is always a price, for everything. He had made contacts with people in Germany and Italy. Because of his rank he could get me across the border into Hungary. But I must take this stuff with me. I was paid some money before I left, some more in Hamburg, where I delivered three bags. These three must go to an address in Bayswater. I phoned there this morning, while I was out for my walk. Very English voice, very upper class! They haven't given me much money of course, a fraction of what it's worth. The KGB Colonel had his cut, for recruiting me. We got to Budapest, and separated. I hope I never see him again . . . Who can ever be sure of anything. That is all, my friends. There is no more to say. I have told no one any of this ever before, except once an absolute stranger, alone in an all night train. Now you may pour your contempt upon me, for the right reasons, not the wrong ones!

Irish
young/middle-aged

The Rivals

Richard Brinsley Sheridan

This eighteenth century comedy of manners was first performed
at the Theatre Royal, Covent Garden in 1775. It is set in Bath
and revolves around the rivals for the hand of the lovely Lydia
Languish and the subsequent intrigues leading up to a comic
attempt at a duel, arranged by SIR LUCIUS O'TRIGGER – a penni-
less Irish baronet. Meanwhile, Lydia's middle-aged Aunt, Mrs
Malaprop, has developed a passion for SIR LUCIUS and is sending him love letters via her unscrupulous maid, Lucy, who has
persuaded the baronet that he is corresponding not with the
Aunt, but with the Niece.

In this scene, Lucy brings SIR LUCIUS the latest letter from
his 'dear Delia', making sure that she receives her usual reward.

Published by A & C Black, London

Act 2, scene 2

SIR LUCIUS

Hah! my little embassadress – upon my conscience I have been looking for you; I have been on the South Parade this half-hour . . . Faith! – maybe that was the reason we did not meet; and it is very comical too, how you could go out and I not see you – for I was only taking a nap at the Parade coffee-house, and I chose the window on purpose that I might not miss you . . . and I never dreamt it was so late, till I waked. Well, but my little girl, have you got nothing for me? . . . O faith! I guessed you weren't come empty-handed – well – let me see what the dear creature says . . . (*Gives him a letter*)

(*Reads*) *Sir – there is often a sudden incentive impulse in love, that has a greater induction than years of domestic combination: such was the commotion I felt at the first superfluous view of Sir Lucius O'Trigger.* Very pretty, upon my word. *Female punctuation forbids me to say more; yet let me add, that it will give me joy infallible to find Sir Lucius worthy the last criterion of my affections. – Delia.* Upon my conscience! Lucy, your lady is a great mistress of language. Faith, she's quite the queen of the dictionary! – for the devil a word dare refuse coming at her call – though one would think it was quite out of hearing . . . Faith, she must be very deep read to write this way – though she is a rather arbitrary writer too – for here are a great many poor words pressed into the service of this note, that would get their *habeas corpus* from any court in Christendom. – However, when affection guides the pen, Lucy, he must be a brute who finds fault with the style . . .

O tell her, I'll make her the best husband in the world, and Lady O'Trigger into the bargain! But we must get the old gentlewoman's consent – and do everything fairly.

Arabian
elderly

Ross

Terence Rattigan

First produced at The Haymarket Theatre, London in 1960, it is
the story of Lawrence of Arabia. In this scene the SHEIK AUDA
ABU TAYI tries to persuade Lawrence that it is madness to
attempt to cross the el-Houl desert. AUDA is an elderly man of
great vigour, with a booming voice. He has a natural,
unassumed majesty of presence, which is enhanced by the
splendour of his clothes.

Published in *The Collected Plays of Terence Rattigan* (Volume Three), by Hamish
Hamilton, London

Act 1

AUDA
(*At length.*)
No. It is impossible . . .
El Aurans, it is only a few hours that I have known you, but I understand you better than you think I do. You have said to yourself, Auda is an old man who feeds on flattery. All I need to do to bend him to my will is to remind him of the great feats of his youth. (*Suddenly shouting.*) Of course there was a time when I ignored the word impossible. There was a time, forty years ago, when I led a hundred men across the Southern Desert against ten times that number to avenge an insult to my tribe – and by the great God, avenged it too. That day I killed seven men by my own hand . . . (*Carelessly.*) No doubt some others died of their wounds. Yes, by heaven. That feat was impossible. And there were others too – (*He changes tone.*) But I am no longer twenty and what you suggest is – (*Shouting, off, angrily at someone off stage.*) Kerim! Order that man, on pain of instant decapitation, to stop singing his foolish song. The words are exaggerated and his voice disturbs our thought. (*He turns back to Lawrence.*) There is a boundary between the possible and the impossible that certain exceptional beings such as myself may leap. But there is a boundary between the impossible and a madman's dream – (*The song stops abruptly.*) Thank Allah! There are fifty-six verses to that song – each in praise of either one of my battles or one of my wives. By the dispensation of God the numbers are exactly equal . . .
(*Passionately*). El Aurans, I have no great love for the Turks. Feisal is my friend and I would be his ally. But what are you asking? A march in the worst month of the year across the worst desert in Arabia – el Houl – the desolate – that even the jackals and vultures fear – where the sun can beat a man to madness and where day or night a wind of such scorching dryness can blow that a man's skin is stripped from his body. It is a terrible desert – el Houl – and terrible is not a word that comes lightly to the lips of Auda Abu Tayi.

117

Newcastle/slight
young

Rutherford and Son

Githa Sowerby

Written in 1912 and set in the Potteries in the same period. It is based on the writer's own family, who owned the local glassworks. In this scene, JOHN, the eldest son, learns that his father has pressured Martin, the Works Manager and John's trusted friend, to give him the formula of the invention they had been working on together. He tells Martin to clear out and then turns on his young wife, Mary, accusing her of always holding him back.

Copies may be obtained from the British Library, London

Act 1

JOHN (*almost in tears*)

He knows well enough – (*to Martin*) you knew well enough. You're a thief – you're as bad as he is – you two behind my back. It was mine – the only chance I had. Damn him! damn him! You've done for yourself, that's one thing – you're done for! You'll not get anything out of it now, not a farthing. He's twisted you round his finger, making you think you'd have the pickings, has he? And then thrown you out into the street for a fool and worse. You're done for! . . . You've worked with me, seen it grow. I never thought but to trust you as I trusted myself – and you give it away thinking to make a bit behind my back! You'll not get a farthing now – not a farthing – you're done for . . . Oh, clear out – don't talk to me. By Heaven! I'll be even with him yet . . . (*Martin goes. John suddenly goes to Rutherford's desk and begins pulling out drawers as if searching for something.*) Where's the key, curse it! . . . (*unlocking the cash box*) . . . He's taken all I have. (*He empties the money out on to the desk, his hands shaking.*) Fifteen – twenty – twenty-three. And it's twenty-three thousand he owes me more like, that he's stolen. Is there any more – a sixpence I've missed, that'll help to put us even? Twenty-three quid – curse him! And he stood and talked to me not an hour ago, and all the time he knew! He's mean, that's what he is – mean and petty-minded. No one else could have done it – to go and get at Martin behind my back because he knew I was going to be one too many for him . . . (*Angrily.*) And don't look at me as if I were stealing. It's mine, I tell you. I only wish there were a few thousands – I'd take them! . . . I'm not going to argue – I've done that too long – listening to first one and then another of you. What's come of it? You wouldn't let me go out and sell the thing while it was still mine to sell. I might have been a rich man if I'd been let to go my own way! You were always dragging me back, everything I did – with your talk. Tony – you're perpetually cramming him down my throat, till I'm sick of the very name of the poor little beggar. How much better off is he for your interfering? Give up this and give up that – I've lost everything I ever had by doing as you said. Anybody would have bought it, anybody! and made a fortune out of it – and there it is, lost! gone into Rutherford's, like everything else. Damn the place! damn it! Oh, let him wait! I'll be even with him. I came back once because I was a soft fool – this time I'll starve sooner.

119

American
young/middle-aged

Someone Who'll Watch Over Me

Frank McGuinness

First performed at the Hampstead Theatre, London in 1992.
An Englishman, an Irishman and an American are locked up
together in a cell in the Middle East. ADAM, an American doctor,
has been imprisoned longer than the others. This is his fifth
month and he is fighting to keep his sanity.

Published by Faber & Faber, London

Scene 4

ADAM

I want a pair of jockey shorts. I want to wear my country's greatest contribution to mankind. Fresh, white jockey shorts. A man's underwear. That's why Arabs can't wear them. If their shorts don't have a hole in them, they can't find their dicks. I want a pair of jockey shorts. I want to kill an Arab. Just one. Throw his body down before his mother and father, his wife and kids, and say, I did it, me, the American. Now you can blame me. You are justified in what you do to me. You have deserved this. I want to see their faces fill with hate. True hate. I want that within my power.
(*Silence*).
Fetch me the Koran that I may read of power.
(*He reads from the Koran.*)

> In the name of God, the Merciful, the Compassionate.
> Behold, we sent it down on the Night of Power:
> And what shall teach thee what is the Night of Power?
> The Night of Power is better than a thousand months;
> In it the angels and the Spirit descend,
> By the leave of the Lord, upon every command.
> Peace it is, till the rising of dawn.

(*Silence.*)

> Peace it is, the Night of Power.

(*Silence.*)
Peace in the house, when the foster kids are sleeping. Everyone at peace, except Adam in his head. His head is hot. He forgets his manners. He shoots off his mouth. He hurts. Forgive me, my sisters and my brothers, for doubting if you were sisters and brothers. Forgive me, my foes, for calling you my foes. In your good book lies the way to power and to peace.
(*He kisses the Koran.*)

> I am come into my garden, oh beloved.
> Thou that dwellest in the gardens, the companions
> hearken to thy voice: cause me to hear it.
> Make haste, my beloved, and be thou like to a roe or
> to a young hart upon the mountains of spices . . .
> Ah but my beloved, why do you turn aside from me?
> I am my beloved's, and my beloved is mine.

Irish/Northern Ireland
mid 30s

Someone Who'll Watch Over Me

Frank McGuinness

First performed at the Hampstead Theatre, London in 1992.
An Englishman, an Irishman and an American are locked up
together in a cell in the Middle East. In this scene the American
has been taken out and possibly executed. It is Christmas Day
and, although chained to the wall, EDWARD, a journalist from
Northern Ireland, is exercising and singing carols. As throughout the play, the men pass the time with reminiscences of home,
their moods swinging from hope to despair.

Published by Faber & Faber, London

Scene 8

(*Silence. Edward sings.*)

EDWARD

> Oh come all ye faithful,
> Joyful and triumphant,
> Oh come ye, oh come ye, to Bethlehem.

(*Silence*).

And in the manger is the Christ child. Who has caused all this bother for us. Do you realize that? If we'd been born Muslims, this wouldn't have happened. So it's his fault. Or our father's fault and our mother's fault for believing in him.

(*Edward sings.*)

> Oh come all ye faithful,
> Joyful and triumphant,
> Oh come ye, oh come ye, to Bethlehem.

(*Silence.*)

Passing the time on a Christmas Day. Peace on earth, good will to all men. Peace, what's peace, Michael?

(*Silence.*)

Peace is lying beside a woman. Touching her, by accident, all soft. Smelling her, not stinking like us. Listening to her breathing. That's the only sound she makes, in the peace. Her breath. Listen, listen. Peace together, as she sleeps, and me awake, lovely, lovely. I would press against her belly, and kiss, and I would be happy as a lark. Her legs move as she sleeps and I hold them, and want to lift them and conceive in the morning, on Christmas Day in the morning, in the happy, happy bed, our bed. Wife. Wife. But who's here but you, Michael?

(*Edward laughs.*)

There are times the sight and sound of you disgust me. I can feel a smell off you. Sickening. The sight of you sickens me. The sound of you. I find your smell sickening.

123

American/Southern
middle-aged

Sweet Bird of Youth

Tennessee Williams

Written in 1959, produced in England by the Manchester Experimental Theatre in 1964 and revived at the Palace Theatre, Wat-
ford in 1969. BOSS FINLEY, middle-aged, despotic and
malignant, learns that his daughter has been infected with ven-
ereal disease by Chance Wayne. She announces that she is going
into a convent, but he is determined that nothing is going to
upset his political career. He tells her that she and her brother
Tom must accompany him when he addresses the 'Youth for
Tom Finley' clubs and scotch the rumours of her corruption. He
then goes off to call on his mistress, Miss Lucy.

Published by Secker and Warburg, London

Act 2, scene 1

BOSS (*shouting*)
You ain't going into no convent. This state is a Protestant region
and a daughter in a convent would politically ruin me. Oh, I know,
you took your mama's religion because in your heart you always
wished to defy me. Now, tonight, I'm addressing the 'Youth for
Tom Finley' clubs in the ballroom of the Royal Palms Hotel. My
speech is going out over a national TV network, and Missy, you're
going to march in the ballroom on my arm. You're going to be
wearing the stainless white of a virgin, with a 'Youth for Tom
Finley' button on one shoulder and a corsage of lilies on the other.
You're going to be on the speaker's platform with me, you on one
side of me and Tom Junior on the other, to scotch these rumours
about your corruption. And you're gonna wear a proud happy
smile on your face, you're gonna stare straight out at the crowd in
the ballroom with pride and joy in your eyes. Lookin' at you, all
in white like a virgin, nobody would dare to speak or believe the
ugly stories about you. I'm relying a great deal on this campaign
to bring in young voters for the crusade I'm leading. I'm all that
stands between the South and the black days of Reconstruction.
And you and Tom Junior are going to stand there beside me in the
grand crystal ballroom, as shining examples of white Southern
youth – in danger . . . A lot of people approve of taking violent
action against corrupters. And on all of them that want to adulterate
the pure white blood of the South. Hell, when I was fifteen, I come
down barefoot out of the red clay hills as if the Voice of God called
me. Which it did, I believe. I firmly believe He called me. And
nothing, nobody, nowhere is gonna stop me, never . . . (*He motions
to Charles for gift. Charles hands it to him.*) Thank you, Charles. I'm
gonna pay me an early call on Miss Lucy.
(*A sad, uncertain note has come into his voice on this final line. He turns
and plods wearily, doggedly off at left.*)

African/Moor
young/middle-aged

Titus Andronicus

William Shakespeare

Titus Andronicus is one of Shakespeare's earlier plays and is believed to be written between 1586 and 1594. It is often classified as a Roman play, although it is set in the Late Empire and is very different from any of the others, excelling in tyranny, barbarity and the most appalling horrors and depravities. AARON is a Moor and Queen Tamora's lover, by whom she has a child. He is ambitious, amoral and devoid of any conscience or pity for his victims, although he defends his baby son with his life. He is unrepentant when captured and only regrets that he cannot do a thousand more dreadful deeds.

Act 5, scene 1

AARON

> Ay, that I had not done a thousand more.
> Even now I curse the day – and yet, I think,
> Few come within the compass of my curse –
> Wherein I did not some notorious ill:
> As kill a man, or else devise his death;
> Ravish a maid, or plot the way to do it;
> Accuse some innocent, and forswear myself;
> Set deadly enmity between two friends;
> Make poor men's cattle break their necks;
> Set fire on barns and hay-stacks in the night,
> And bid the owners quench them with their tears.
> Oft have I digg'd up dead men from their graves,
> And set them upright at their dear friends' door
> Even when their sorrows almost was forgot,
> And on their skins, as on the bark of trees,
> Have with my knife carved in Roman letters
> 'Let not your sorrow die, though I am dead'.
> Tut, I have done a thousand dreadful things
> As willingly as one would kill a fly;
> And nothing grieves me heartily indeed
> But that I cannot do ten thousand more.

The Actors' Theatre School
32 Exeter Road
London NW2 4SB
tel: 0181-450 0371
fax: 0181-450 1057

Offstage Theatre and Film Bookshop
37 Chalk Farm Road
London NW1 8AJ
tel: 0171-485 4996
fax: 0171-916 8046

The British Library
96 Euston Road
London NW1 2DB
tel: 0171-412 7676 (printed material)
    0171-412 7513 (manuscript material)

Victoria Library
160 Buckingham Palace Road
London SW1 9UD
tel: 0171-798 2187

Royal Academy of Dramatic Art
62/64 Gower Street
London WC1E 6ED
tel: 0171-636 7076

London Academy of Music and
Dramatic art (LAMDA)
Tower House
226 Cromwell Road
London SW5 0SR
tel: 0171-373 9883

Drama Studio London
Grange Court
1 Grange Road
London W5 5QN
tel: 0181-579 3897

American Academy of Dramatic Art
120 Madison Avenue
New York, NY 10016
tel: 212-686 9244

The following have kindly granted permission for the reprinting of copyright material.

Blood Relations by Sharon Pollock
From *Blood Relations and Other Plays*. Reprinted by permission of NeWest Publishers Limited, Edmonton.

Boesman and Lena by Athol Fugard
From Fugard's *Selected Plays* published by Oxford University Press 1987. Used by permission of Oxford University Press.

Breezeblock Park by Willy Russell
© 1978 by Willy Russell, published by Samuel French Ltd. Reproduced by permission. All rights whatsoever in this play are strictly reserved and application for performance etc., should be made before rehearsal to Casarotto Ramsay Ltd, National House, 60–66 Wardour Street, London W1V 4ND. No performance may be given unless a licence has been obtained.

The Cherry Orchard by Anton Chekhov
Extract from Act III (pp 383–384) from *The Cherry Orchard* from *Plays* by Anton Chekhov, translated by Elisaveta Fen (Penguin Classics 1951) copyright © Elisaveta Fen 1951. Reproduced by permission of Penguin Books Ltd. Performing rights controlled by The Society of Authors.

Daughters of Venice by Don Taylor
© 1992 by Don Taylor, published by Samuel French Ltd. All rights whatsoever in this play are strictly

reserved and application for performance etc. should be made before rehearsal to Casarotto Ramsay Ltd, National House, 60–66 Wardour Street, London W1V 4ND. No performance may be given unless a licence has been obtained.

Dead Dad Dog by John McKay
From *Dead Dad Dog* by John McKay from *Scot-Free* edited by Alastair Cameron published by Nick Hern Books. © 1990 by John McKay. Reproduced by permission of Nick Hern Books.

Death of a Salesman by Arthur Miller
Two extracts from *Death of a Salesman* by Arthur Miller. UK: Copyright © 1948, 1949, 1951, 1952 by Arthur Miller, renewed 1975, 1976, 1979, 1980; reproduced by permission of the author c/o Rogers, Coleridge & White Ltd., 20 Powis Mews, London W11 1JN in association with International Creative Management, 40 West 57th Street, New York, NY 10019, USA.

The Devil's Disciple by George Bernard Shaw
Reprinted by permission of The Society of Authors on behalf of the Bernard Shaw Estate. Published by Penguin Books.

Diff'rent by Eugene O'Neill
From *Collected Plays of Eugene O'Neill*, published by Jonathan Cape Limited a

129

performance may be given unless a licence has been obtained.